YEOVIL

THE HIDDEN HISTORY

Leslie Brooke (left) and Leonard Hayward (right) pictured at the launch of *The Book of Yeovil* in 1978. In the centre are Ernest Batty and John Goodchild.

Dedication

This book is dedicated to the memory of Leonard Hayward and Leslie Brooke, who both did so much to uncover Yeovil's hidden history.

YEOVIL
THE HIDDEN HISTORY

edited by

BRIAN AND MOIRA GITTOS

TEMPUS

This book contains maps based on copyright digital map data
owned and supplied by Harper Collins Cartographic
and is used with permission.

First published 2004

Tempus Publishing Ltd
The Mill, Brimscombe Port
Stroud, Gloucestershire GL5 2QG
www.tempus-publishing.com

British Library Cataloguing in Publication Data.
A catalogue record for this book is available from the British Library.

ISBN 0 7524 3121 8

Typesetting and origination by Tempus Publishing.
Printed and bound in Great Britain.

CONTENTS

PREFACE

2004 marks 50 years since the foundation of the Yeovil Archaeological and Local History Society (initially known as the Yeovil Archaeological Field Club). This project was conceived as a celebration of what has been achieved over that half century and also to act as an encouragement for the future. It breaks new ground in dealing for the first time with Yeovil from an archaeological perspective. Yeovil presents a face of unashamed modernity and is often perceived as lacking in history, particularly in comparison with Sherborne, its neighbour across the county boundary. Few might have believed that its archaeology was sufficiently rich to warrant a volume in its own right and if this book can assist in counteracting that perception, then it will have achieved its most important objective.

The book highlights particular aspects rather than attempting to be comprehensive but, for those wishing to pursue the subject further, there is a Bibliography and an Appendix listing the major archaeological activities which have taken place in the locality. A map of the town centre at the end of the nineteenth century is also appended, for those less familiar with its layout before the Quedam and Queensway. There are seven essays, all by Society members, which reflect their own interests, expertise and areas of research. This brings with it a variety of styles and view points but also the added freshness and depth which comes from dealing with a favourite subject. The range of topics is very wide, covering such disparate matters as prehistoric gold, a Roman milestone, medieval churches, town centre archaeology, the Yeovil Tithe map and Second World War air-raid shelters. There should be something to suit all tastes. The remit of Yeovil's hidden history has been interpreted rather liberally in some cases, particularly with regard to the chapter on the Norman church at Stoke sub Hamdon. However, some exciting conclusions have emerged from the YALHS's current project on the church and it also paints a picture of some aspects of life in this part of Somerset in the years immediately following the Norman Conquest. This is not a well understood period of Yeovil's history and it is therefore of particular value.

One of the benefits of putting together a work of this kind is the new discoveries which always result from the endeavour. Examples include the surviving traces of Second World War camouflage on a building in the centre of the town; the realisation that many housing blocks around Yeovil perpetuate old field boundaries and the fact that St John's once enjoyed the services of an Archpriest. However, it is the enjoyment of the reader which is the objective and if the individual writers' enthusiasm comes through, then the book will be all the more interesting for it.

Many people have been involved to a greater or lesser extent, with the process of putting together the material for this book and our warmest thanks go to them all. Special mention must be made of the help given by the following: Marjorie Brooke for the loan of original drawings and maps from her husband's collection and giving her permission to reproduce many examples; Dr John Blair of The Queen's College, Oxford and Dr Helen Gittos for valued comments on aspects of Chapter 3; David Dawson for advice on the pottery from the Library Site and assistance with exhibits in the County Museum; Steve Minnitt of the Somerset County Museum for providing the illustration of the East Coker mosaic and help with items in the collection; David Bromwich of the Local Studies Library, Taunton for help on many aspects, particularly tithe maps; the staff of the Museum of South Somerset for making available some of the archaeological material; Hugh Prudden for loan of the illustration of St Michael's Hill; Fred Balham for assistance with Westland archive material; Porter Dodson for access to the Chantry; the staff of Yeovil Reference Library; the churchwardens of both St John's Yeovil and St Mary Stoke sub Hamdon and Alan Gittos for photography.

It was extremely sad that Leslie Brooke died in December 2003. He would have enjoyed the finished product and had already been involved through the loan of important material including his slide of the gold torc (cover) and his unpublished manuscript history of the town to 1900. The loss of a valued friend and such a knowledgeable historian of Yeovil could not have occurred at a more unfortunate time as far as this project was concerned but his enthusiasm and wisdom have been ever present in the minds of the editors and authors throughout its completion. It was felt that the most appropriate response in the circumstances was to dedicate this book not just to the Society's founder, Leonard Hayward, as was the original intention, but also to Leslie Brooke. Between them they laid the necessary foundations not only for the present volume but for our understanding of Yeovil's history.

CHAPTER 1

YEOVIL'S ARCHAEOLOGY

Brian and Moira Gittos

INTRODUCTION

In the early hours of Sunday 22 September 1935, a disastrous fire destroyed Yeovil's Town Hall *(1)*. Although it was a prominent building in the centre of the town, it was not of any great architectural merit, nor was it of any antiquity (built 1849). However, in that conflagration was consumed some of the evidence which charted Yeovil's history. There had been major fires in the town previously, notably in 1449 and 1640 and important records had been lost during repairs to the Tolle Hall, following its partial collapse, in the late eighteenth century. The destruction of the Town Hall was thus only one in a series of disasters which have swept away the town's historical records. Other Somerset towns, such as Bridgwater and Wells, are fortunate in the extent and quality of their archives but for Yeovil, the archaeological record assumes a greater significance in attempting to piece together its past. Unfortunately, the first proper archaeological investigation within the medieval borough is still awaited but over the last 70 years or so, a great variety of information has been gleaned from small-scale activities.

BEGINNINGS

During the nineteenth century, a growing interest in antiquities and archaeology spawned the establishment of county archaeological societies across the country. The Somerset Archaeological and Natural History Society (SANHS), founded in 1849, was one such. More locally, such interests were amply demonstrated by the activities of successive members of the Walter family at

1 Yeovil's Town Hall about 1910, from a sketch by Leslie Brooke. © *Marjorie Brooke*

Stoke sub Hamdon *(colour plate 8)*. They investigated many aspects of the archaeology of Stoke sub Hamdon and Ham Hill itself. Their collection of artefacts from the hill fort, some of which can be seen in the Somerset County Museum at Taunton, was the foundation for understanding the monument and its significance. The inhabitants of Yeovil were somewhat more reticent in embracing this new interest. It was not until some 100 years after the foundation of SANHS that the town's own society, the Yeovil Archaeological Field Club, had its inaugural meeting (1954). Although collections of interesting antiquities were displayed at SANHS meetings in Yeovil in 1853 and 1886, a serious attempt to establish a museum in the town can only be traced back to the early twentieth century. It took the form of a miscellany of objects displayed in the former billiard room of No.28 Kingston. This assemblage included many items unconnected with the town, such as Zulu shields and spears but also a few which were to form part of the museum's permanent collection.

In 1909 a fine Bronze Age gold torc was discovered among imported topsoil in a garden on Hendford Hill. A coroner's inquest held in the Town Hall determined that since there was no evidence it had been deliberately hidden by its owner, it could not be considered Treasure Trove. Seven years later, a hoard of Roman coins was found in Seaton Road and this was the first indication of the important site at Westland Road, which was excavated in the 1920s. These momentous events in Yeovil's archaeological history are dealt with in Chapter 2. Their role in raising local awareness of the subject must have been profound and it found expression in 1928 with the formal establishment of a municipal museum above the new Borough Library in King George Street. Its purpose was to display the Roman finds from Westland but it also included material which had been displayed at No.28 Kingston. Much of the impetus for the new museum came from an enthusiastic local councillor, Alderman Mitchelmore, who had been deeply involved in the activities at Westland and now became the museum's first honorary curator. However, William Wyndham generously donated £2,000 to enable the idea to be realised. The museum was installed in a new home in Hendford Manor Hall in 1965 and the collection was redisplayed. Originally built as a coach house for Hendford Manor in the late eighteenth century, this is an attractive two-storied building, and is still home to the collection, now renamed the Museum of South Somerset.

Wyndham also founded and endowed the Wyndham Trust to encourage the boys of Yeovil School to take an active interest in archaeology. The Trust took the form of a school museum and a regular series of lectures by visiting speakers on archaeological topics. Since then there have been major changes to the structure of education in the town but, after more than 70 years, the work of the Trust continues, overseeing the collection (now divided amongst the local secondary schools) and providing grants to promote history and archaeology to local students in a more exciting way.

POST SECOND WORLD WAR

When in 1945 Leonard Hayward came to Yeovil as Senior History Master at Yeovil School, he built on the foundation of the Wyndham Trust and formed the Yeovil School Archaeological Society. This was to have far-reaching consequences since, in order to provide practical experience for the boys, some digging was required. Initially the site of the Priory at Montacute was favoured, but in April 1945 a farm worker driving a tractor noticed some interesting features in a field just north of Lufton village. Examination confirmed the presence of a Roman building and in the following year, the Yeovil School Archaeological Society set about an excavation. The venture was highly successful, the building proving to be a villa with many well-preserved mosaics and an impressive octagonal bath house (revealed in the first season). Digging at Lufton carried on until 1952 and the momentum was maintained in April 1954, when the Society began work on a second Roman villa, at Ilchester Mead (south-west of modern Ilchester).

1954 was to prove a pivotal year in charting Yeovil's archaeology. It was the centenary of the foundation of the borough and the Town Council appointed a celebrations committee to organise an exhibition of local history at Hendford Manor Hall. To coincide with the exhibition a short history of the town was written, entitled *The Borough of Yeovil*. This was compiled by John Goodchild, who was editor of the *Western Gazette* at the time, with the assistance of Leonard Hayward and Ernest Batty, Yeovil Borough Librarian and Curator of the Wyndham Museum. Clearly the time was right for creating a new body to act as a focus for this burgeoning interest in archaeology and local history. In October, Leonard Hayward called a meeting at Yeovil School to discuss the possibilities and from this was born the Yeovil and District Archaeological Field Club (changing in 1959, to become the Yeovil Archaeological and Local History Society). The new Society was formed to identify and excavate archaeological sites in the locality, publish the results and organise a lecture programme. Early speakers included Professor Barry Cunliffe (Iron Age and Roman specialist and excavator of Hengistbury Head, Danebury and Bath); Philip Rahtz (excavator of the Anglo-Saxon palace at Cheddar and, later, Professor of Archaeology at York University); Harold St George Gray (archaeological pioneer who conducted major excavations on the Glastonbury and Meare lake villages) and Leslie Alcock (excavator of South Cadbury hill fort).

The Ilchester Mead excavation revealed remains from a third-century villa arranged around a courtyard (the equivalent of a modern working farm). The site did not replicate the excitement of Lufton, although two principal campaigns were mounted, both under Leonard Hayward's direction in the 1950s and '60s, finishing in 1972. The report appeared a decade later in 1982. The work was undertaken by the boys of Yeovil School and the girls of Yeovil High School, together with members of the Society. Between these campaigns, attention turned back to Lufton, perhaps prompted by a sense of unfinished business. For the first year of this campaign, which spanned 1960-63, excavation proceeded at both Lufton and Ilchester Mead but for the next two, all effort was concentrated at Lufton since the landowner was keen to see an end to the activity. The work at Lufton, in contrast to the earlier campaign, was directed to the more domestic areas of the building. It yielded evidence of a comfortable corridor villa, with under-floor heating and mosaic pavements. It also showed how the use of the building had changed in the fourth century, with an increase in industrial activity (see Chapter 2).

Towards the end of the initial excavations at Ilchester Mead, another Society member proposed tackling a third Roman villa at Chessels in West Coker parish, close to the Yeovil boundary. George Aitkin, Headmaster of East Coker School, persuaded the Society to apply to the Ministry of Works for permission to excavate, since this site was already a scheduled monument. This was readily granted and, in a small area, three 8ft (2.4m) squares were opened. The area produced only the footings of one wall and two robber trenches but a considerable quantity of pottery and 12 coins (late third to the end of the fourth century) were also found. Officials at the Ministry were very circumspect about granting permission for a further season, which would have ranged more widely over the site, and in the event it did not take place. A brief report was produced and a few duplicated copies made.

THE GEORGE INN

In 1960, the Borough Council took a decision in principle to accept the owner's plan to demolish the last remaining secular medieval building in the town. The future of The George in Middle Street had been under debate for some years, since it was the last constriction in the course of the main road through the town. The plan was controversial, and the building is still remembered with affection by Yeovilians, but the decision was upheld by a Public Enquiry. Demolition took place in April 1962. Members of the YALHS took a leading role in recording the building, through measured drawings and photographs, during the process. The Society had not previously been involved with either the recording of a standing building or rescue archaeology but the surviving records are evidence of their success. The George had originally been built as a private dwelling, around the middle of the fifteenth century and only later converted to a small inn. It was a timber-framed building, with a jettied upper storey and of a style rarely found in the west of England. So-called Wealden houses are a feature of medieval vernacular architecture in the south-east with The George being recognised at the time as the most westerly example of this distinctive building type. Wealden houses have a central hall open to the roof, with two-storied bays at either end which are jettied, so that seen from the front the upper part of the hall appears recessed. The name 'Wealden' derives from the Weald of Kent, where the type is most common. A two-light window frame was donated to the museum and The George passed into history. Ironically, the next decade saw the building of an inner ring road (Queensway) which enabled Middle Street to be pedestrianised, but it came too late to save The George.

FURTHER EXCAVATIONS

Before the conclusion of work at Ilchester Mead in 1972, a new project began a few miles north-west at Catsgore. The work extended to four seasons, from 1970-73, and proved to be of great archaeological significance, with a substantial portion of a Romano-British village being uncovered. Even today it is still among the best understood of such sites in the country. Directed by Roger Leech and funded by bodies including the Department of the Environment, it is described as having been carried out on behalf of the Yeovil Archaeological and Local History Society. The role of the YALHS in the project was acknowledged when the final report was published in 1982.

1972 saw the publication of the 1960-63 excavations at Lufton, in the *Proceedings of the Somerset Archaeological and Natural History Society* and, at last, some archaeology within the town itself. New premises for Marks and Spencer were to be built between Middle Street and Vicarage Street, and Leonard Hayward conducted a watching brief. No report appears to have been published and there are only a handful of clues that the site did produce important material. A few sherds of eleventh-century pottery were deposited in the museum, along with a medieval bung-hole pot and a goblet of similar date. After 18 years of the YALHS's existence, archaeological knowledge of the town itself had advanced very little.

PUBLICATIONS

Leonard Hayward decided, in 1975, to step down after 21 years as Chairman of the YALHS. The position was filled by Isobel Rendell, a teacher who had wide archaeological experience, including excavation at Glastonbury Abbey with Raleigh Radford. Several new members joined the committee and this heralded a change of emphasis in the Society's activities. Leslie Brooke was graphic designer of the *Western Gazette* and had the combined talents of artist and historian. He had already published the standard work on Somerset Newspapers and was deeply interested in Yeovil's history. Bill Chapman had wide-ranging interests and a love of archaeology. He was involved in the discovery of Anglo-Saxon pottery at Yew Tree Close in 1975 and the deserted medieval village of Barrow (in the parish of Odcombe). The following year, the Society embarked on a new venture and on 27 March staged 'Symposium '76', jointly with the Yeovil and District Natural History Society. Eight speakers took part, 184 tickets were sold and the Symposium did much to raise awareness of the Society, both locally and elsewhere in the county. Further indications of the new direction that the YALHS was to take came in 1978, when Leslie Brooke published *The Book of Yeovil*. Although not a Society publication, it set the scene for an interest in publication, which has continued to the present day. Unlike the *Borough of Yeovil*, 24 years previously, Leslie Brooke's approach was to make maximum use of illustrations, including a number of his own pen and ink sketches, which brought to life lost buildings and townscapes. In this new climate, a decision was made that the Society should undertake a programme of publishing and a Publications Sub-Committee was set up. The process began with the first of a series of booklets, usually known by its short title *The Romans*, which came out in the same year. Thereafter one booklet was published each year until 1981: *Street Names in Yeovil* (1979), *Bygone Yeovil* (1980) and *Yeovil: the Changing Scene* (1981).

This remarkable burst of activity had its most far-reaching effect when Leslie Brooke, the founding editor, launched the Society's journal *Chronicle* in September 1978. From this point, there was a vehicle to record events as they happened (initially twice each year) and also a means of reporting work undertaken by members, some of which might otherwise have been consigned to oblivion. *Chronicle* is still in publication and many of the subjects considered at length in this book were first aired in its pages. A full set of the journal is held in the Tite Collection in Yeovil's Reference Library.

Hands-on archaeology returned to the fore in 1981 when the Ilchester Flood Prevention Scheme disturbed a great concentration of mostly Roman deposits. A well-preserved bronze coin of Aurelian (AD 270-275) was one of many items recovered from the spoil heaps *(2)*. Although excavations were no longer on the YALHS agenda, a new project was launched in September 1979, which required a great deal of physical effort and commitment. This was the Tintinhull Project, which focused on the medieval parish church and the churchyard of this neighbouring community and likely former 'daughter' church to Yeovil St John's (see Chapter 3). The work was wide-ranging but the main elements were a photographic survey of the building, its fixtures and fittings (undertaken by Marjorie and Leslie Brooke) and a full record of the churchyard monuments (including a surveyed plan) led by Pat Knight. A copy of the churchyard survey results was deposited with the Somerset and Dorset Family History Society library. A similar project is

2 Obverse and reverse of a Roman coin of the Emperor Aurelian (AD 270-275) found on the spoil heaps of the Ilchester Flood Prevention Scheme in 1981. Coins of this emperor are rarely found on British sites. © *Alan Gittos*

currently in progress at Stoke sub Hamdon, one aspect of which has provided Chapter 4 of this book.

THE QUEDAM DEVELOPMENT AND ITS CONSEQUENCES

After years of piecemeal alterations to the town centre, Yeovil underwent its first major redevelopment in 1983/4, with the building of the Quedam shopping precinct and its associated multi-storey car park and delivery area. It was centred on the former Vicarage Street and stretched northward as far as Market Street, encompassing a section of the later medieval town. In this large area, there was almost complete destruction of the archaeology but no investigation was carried out. The only archaeology took place in late September 1983, when workmen uncovered a brick tomb containing a lead-lined coffin, which was reported to the coroner. The coffin was removed to the mortuary at Yeovil District Hospital where an examination was undertaken by Leonard Hayward. It contained the skeleton of an adult male of about 40 years of age, estimated to be some 6ft (1.8m) tall. The teeth were well preserved and the hair survived (3). The tomb was found on the site of the Unitarian chapel which had stood on the north side of Vicarage Street. When the chapel was built it was set back from the road and the tomb probably occupied part of the space at the front (4). It had been an elaborate and expensive burial, since in addition to the brick vault, the lead coffin had been inside a wooden coffin (only a few fragments of which remained). Clearly it was the tomb of a person of some importance and Leonard Hayward suggested the most likely candidate was Robert Batten who was born around 1748 and was still alive in 1779. The bones were buried in Yeovil cemetery, together with the skulls of two adult females which had been found nearby.

The destruction of so much of Yeovil's archaeology, without any official attempt to record what was being lost, came as a serious shock. It was as a direct consequence of this, that when work began on the new library three years later, the YALHS became involved and made strenuous efforts to record the evidence as it was revealed. Looking back, it is easy to see that what followed stemmed from a combination of elements coming together at the right time. These included the availability of people to do the work, outstanding co-operation on the part of the contractors and their workmen and a freedom of action unthinkable in the light of modern legislation and litigation. The Library Site lasted for two seasons and is the largest archaeological project to have taken place in the town centre (for details see Chapter 5). When work on the Library Site was at its height in June 1986 a redevelopment of Nos 56 and 58 Middle Street was briefly observed. This involved some deep excavations to remove a small cellar. The clean, sandy soil was seen to be almost totally devoid of features and artefacts. There was nothing to indicate any previous

3 Right Skeleton at Yeovil District Hospital after discovery on the site of the Quedam development. Believed to be Robert Batten who was living in the 1770s and would have been buried at the Unitarian chapel which formerly stood on the site. © *B. and M. Gittos*

4 Below The former Unitarian chapel in Vicarage Street, from a sketch by Leslie Brooke. © *Marjorie Brooke*

occupation. Concurrent with the second year on the library site, in 1987, a similar situation arose across the road, in Petters Way (also Chapter 5). Shortly afterwards (November 1987), some recording was done in Belmont Street, when the relief road was put through the south-eastern side of the town. It crossed the site of Frogg Mill, which may well be the mill mentioned in Domesday Book (1086) as part of the manor of Hendford and worth 10 shillings. The work uncovered a large, mostly stone-lined chamber which had been dredged and the silt dumped on one side. It was an evil, oily, mess that repelled any examination of its possible archaeological riches. However, a cylindrical object was recovered from the very edge of the heap *(colour plate 5)*. It proved to be an Anglo-Saxon baluster *(colour plate 3)* and a possible context for this important stone is explained in Chapter 3. Also in 1987, assistance was given to a family in East Coker who had discovered pottery and stones whilst digging foundations for an extension. The evidence pointed to a medieval house having occupied the site and further work in 1990 confirmed this, with the opening of an additional trench on the property next door. The house seemed to have been demolished in the sixteenth century and although only small areas were excavated they produced some remarkable finds. A complete fifteenth-century rondel dagger *(5)* was unearthed and a 'fist-full' of crumpled window leading still retaining a decayed fragment of its original glass *(6)*. It had evidently been a wealthy residence.

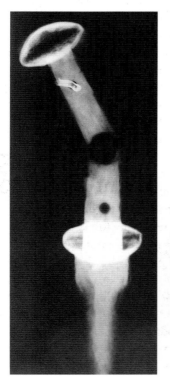

5 Left Photograph of an X-ray image of an iron rondel dagger found on the site of a medieval house in East Coker.
© *B. and M. Gittos*

6 Below A 'fist full' of lead cames from a painted glass window excavated from the site of a medieval house in East Coker and believed to be associated with its demolition.
© *B. and M. Gittos*

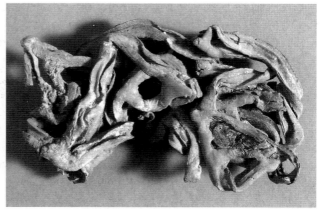

THE ARCHAEOLOGICAL UNIT

It is clear from Appendix II that 1987 was a time of intense activity. This burden was being carried by very few people and was unsustainable. In response, the YALHS set up an archaeological unit as a sub-group of the Society in February 1988. There was enthusiastic support for the new venture within the Society and a generous grant of £500 was received from the Town Council. The first task of the fledgling Unit was rather different from what had gone before. It was to record the worked stones at Church House, just south of the parish church. Construction work in the grounds of the property (then occupied by Batten & Co) involved the demolition of a small building which had stood in the south-east corner of the forecourt. It had a highly irregular ground plan and two entrances, at different levels, which allowed access to an adjacent building. Its function was unclear and no illustrations of it are known. However, the worked stones which had been incorporated into it proved very interesting (7). Two fourteenth-century unglazed window heads and their bases were the best preserved (8) and a pair of these was set up as a recess in the porch which replaced the demolished building. One stone was part of the head of a small, simple, round arched window and could have been from an early building (see Chapter 3). Of a different nature again was the photographic recording carried out at the former police station known as the Town House in Union Street (9). In January 1989 it was about to be modernised to provide accommodation for the Town Council. It still retained many period fittings relating to its nineteenth-century origins and the opportunity was taken to record the building as it then stood. As well as undertaking assignments such as this, the Unit held regular meetings in the CVS offices at Petters House, now fully functioning on the spot where the eighteenth-century rubbish pits had been investigated in 1987 (Chapter 5).

Also in January 1989, building work commenced on another town centre plot. This was at Lloyds Bank on the north side of the High Street, which was being totally reconstructed, leaving only the original façade. It was arranged for the Unit to carry out a watching brief. Difficult conditions meant that it was only feasible for one or two people to be on site at a time and they could only work during lunch breaks and after hours. In the event, it was only possible to examine a small area at the end of the plot furthest from the High Street. Four rubbish pits were identified but no obvious structures. The finds included a high proportion of bone and oyster shells and only a limited quantity of pottery. However, the pot suggested that one of the pits was probably of late medieval date and three eighteenth-century clay pipes were recovered from another. The site foreman pointed out the approximate positions of two wells that had been uncovered elsewhere on the site and back-filled with concrete. A notable feature was the high wall along the boundary with the grounds of Church House. This delineated a sharp difference in ground level, being very much higher on the Church House side. The significance of this is dealt with in Chapter 3.

7 Recording the worked stones at Church House, Church Street, in 1988. © *B. and M. Gittos*

8 Left Fourteenth-century window head from the stone recording exercise in the grounds of Church House in 1988. The scale is marked in inches. © *B. and M. Gittos*

9 Below Yeovil Town House in Union Street, which was formerly the police station, built in 1849. From a sketch by Leslie Brooke. © *Marjorie Brooke*

A year after it was formed, the Archaeological Unit was requested to provide manpower for work at Nethercoombe Farm on the outskirts of Sherborne. This derelict farm had been purchased by the Dorset Historic Buildings Trust, in order to refurbish it. It had traditionally been associated with a lost chapel dedicated to St Emerenciana (the patron saint of earthquakes!). This added interest to the project, which involved excavating both internally and externally. Staff from the Dorset County Archaeological Department led the work, which continued intermittently until August 1989. It was initially well supported but proved to be disappointing and enthusiasm waned. The potential of the site was not fully realised due to severe restrictions on the permitted depth of excavation. This meant that digging was effectively confined to the most recent post-medieval layers and the earlier history was not exposed.

A major opportunity was missed in 1991 when Yeovil's football ground was redeveloped to provide a new store for Tesco. On the southern edge of the area, there had been a small Calvinist burial ground known as 'Paradise'. The bodies were exhumed by a firm of local undertakers in a non-archaeological manner. It had been agreed in principle for the YALHS to conduct a watching brief on the site as a whole but health and safety considerations meant that, in practice, this proved too difficult. Later in the year, observations were made on the course of a new water pipeline beside the A37, south of Ilchester, with some unexpected results. In one location there was a concentration of pottery and pieces of clay pipe. From amongst some 21 bowls, 15 are marked 'ID' which suggests that the elusive 'ID' pipe maker, responsible for many of the pipes found around the town, may have been associated with Ilchester rather than Yeovil. The following summer the Unit supported an excavation, led by Richard Coleman-Smith, on one of the post-medieval pottery kilns near Donyatt. This proved to be a very worthwhile experience, since it involved members of the Unit with material of a type frequently encountered in Yeovil.

10 Medieval mortar carved from blue lias limestone, discovered when a wall was partially demolished in South Street.
© B. and M. Gittos

A chance find from a partly demolished wall in South Street was a corner of a medieval mortar carved, unusually, from blue lias limestone *(10)*.

In the early 1990s it became more and more difficult for local societies such as the YALHS to undertake rescue archaeology but there were special circumstances which enabled the Society to mount a modest series of excavations at Stoford in 1994 and 1997. A Society member who already had outline planning permission for house building on his extensive garden in Stoford, invited the YALHS to carry out some trial trenching. The historical record suggests that Stoford was conceived in the thirteenth century as a new planned town but, prior to the YALHS activity, there was no archaeological evidence to support this. Its task was, therefore, something of a challenge and the results were rewarding, even if not spectacular. The work proceeded at a somewhat leisurely pace, which meant that very little was missed. As a consequence much medieval pottery was recovered, together with a quantity of worked flints. The pottery is mostly small abraded sherds, ranging from the thirteenth to the fifteenth centuries, with a small number of earlier date. The only feature discovered was a medieval ditch which had silted up, been re-cut and finally filled in and capped with clay. From its location and orientation it is likely to have been a property boundary, perhaps dividing two of the burgage plots. This limited evidence at last gives some credence to the existence of medieval Stoford.

THE INFLUENCE OF PPG 16

The reasons for the sharp decline in YALHS archaeology in the early 1990s were many but, undoubtedly, PPG 16 played a major part. Planning Policy Guidance No.16 (PPG 16) was issued by the Government in 1990, with the aim of ensuring that local authorities could require developers to fund investigations, wherever there was good cause to believe that significant archaeology existed. Under this system, which is still current, planning applications are referred to the County Council for comment, from the Historic Environment Service. They are checked against known and likely areas of archaeological potential. If in an area of interest, they are referred back to the District Council, with a recommendation that approval should be conditional upon an appropriate level of archaeological work being carried out. Sometimes work may also be requested to assess the site, before a final decision is made on the application. The regulations and timescales for this type of archaeology are such that it is extremely difficult for amateur societies to participate. As a result, the great majority of town centre archaeology undertaken since the advent of PPG 16, has been the work of professionals. These investigations have been scattered across the town, rather than being positioned to answer specific questions, since they can only take place where development is planned. Even so, they have sometimes produced interesting results. Perhaps surprisingly, in view of the concentration of material at the Library Site, Petters Way and Lloyds Bank, several areas in the town centre have provided either no evidence, or nothing datable earlier than the nineteenth century.

Observation in 1999 at Nos 44 and 46 Middle Street saw nothing but the underlying natural, corroborating the similar impression from Nos 56 and 58 Middle Street (see above). In South Street, at the Town House (1999), although there was evidence of eighteenth and nineteenth-century rubbish pits, the layer containing modern material and brick lay directly on the natural. In Princes Street (1998), on the western side at No.37 (currently Pinewood Studio), there was a cobbled yard, laid on top of late nineteenth-century pottery, without anything datable below. Close to the areas already demonstrated to have earlier development, the story was rather different. Work behind The Mermaid, in 1999, provided undated evidence of leather dressing and a substantial amount of eighteenth-century pottery. Investigations of the Baptist church site in South Street (2002), found the remains of drystone walls and two pits which contained building debris and pottery spanning the seventeenth to the mid-eighteenth century. In the same area there was also medieval pottery, probably of the thirteenth and fourteenth centuries. A small development at Church House (1998) found foundations of walls and rubbish pits, containing pottery from the sixteenth, seventeenth and eighteenth centuries.

There have been a number of professional watching briefs in the development areas to the west of the town, particularly at Alvington and Brympton. Radiocarbon dates from the Bronze Age settlement at Alvington suggest 1900–1100 BC. Elsewhere evidence of a farmstead, which was probably occupied throughout the late Iron Age and Roman periods with worked flints and Roman pottery, has been found. The course of a pipeline put through past Odcombe in 1996 revealed traces of prehistory over most of its route, also cutting Bronze Age pits and a medieval settlement. By contrast, work in Horsey Lane, Lysander Road and Preston Road has found nothing. It is also surprising that work in two areas adjacent to the known Roman site at Westland (1992 and 2003) could add nothing. However, in Freedom Avenue in 2001, traces of a possible Roman settlement were uncovered, a find made all the more interesting since this is adjacent to the quarry area where several Roman burials were found at the beginning of the twentieth century.

Although the YALHS is no longer directly involved in the aspects of archaeology covered by PPG 16, the Society takes part in consultations about significant developments and occasionally tackles small recording opportunities, when they arise. One such resulted from refurbishment of the Chantry in Church Path in 1998. A dilapidated stone wall just to the north of the building was taken down and, in a similar manner to the stones at Church House ten years previously, the YALHS recorded the worked stone. There was nothing to indicate reuse of particularly old material but two pieces of Ham stone were

11 Ham stone post base from a demolished wall adjacent to the Chantry. © *B. and M. Gittos*

found to have shallow, square recesses *(11)*. These may well have acted as bases for wooden posts. Early illustrations of the Borough show the Under Bow, a jettied shopfront, treated in this manner. The Chantry wall stones are of two sizes, neither of which would have been suitable for a major building. Also in 1998, the Society embarked on a long-term project to study the parish church at Stoke sub Hamdon. Building on the experience of the Tintinhull Church Project, this is intended to be a thorough investigation of the church, its graveyard and their historical and landscape contexts. Much of the churchyard has been recorded, the study of the flora has been published and a geophysical survey of one particularly interesting area carried out. Much has been learnt about the background history and the building itself has been examined in considerable detail. Some of the fruits of this endeavour are the subject of Chapter 4.

HISTORIC ENVIRONMENT RECORD

To bring this history right up to date, mention should made of an excellent project undertaken by Somerset County Council's Historic Environment Service, which has published the contents of the Somerset Historic Environment Record on the Internet. This is a county-wide database of known sites and places where archaeological finds have been made. Previously called the Sites and Monuments Record, it has been maintained since the early 1980s but in 2002 a grant from the Heritage Lottery Fund allowed this very large and detailed resource to be made available on line. Now known as the Historic Environment Record, Somerset is one of the first counties where this has been done and it can be consulted at www.somerset.gov.uk/her. There is a large number of entries for Yeovil and its environs and key items from the list make up the bulk of Appendix II at the end of this book. The HER online will prove a major resource for the future.

IN CONCLUSION

From this brief survey, it is clear that Yeovil's involvement with archaeology has been shaped by the interests, expertise and, above all, the enthusiasm of particular individuals. Alderman Mitchelmore, in the 1920s and '30s, led the Westland venture and prominently exhibited the results in the new Wyndham Museum. Leonard Hayward excavated two Roman villas, enthused a great many youngsters and launched the Yeovil Archaeological and Local History Society, which still flourishes today. The emphasis changed to publication through the drive and talent of Leslie Brooke, with many books published and the journal *Chronicle* established. More recently the writers have promoted urban archaeology within the town, which continues, albeit under the guise of PPG 16. All these steps can be seen as a cumulative process demonstrated by the material presented here.

From all of these endeavours it is now beyond doubt that the area is archaeologically rich but also that there many aspects of its hidden history which are poorly understood. The kind of piecemeal observation of development sites which has been ongoing in the town for the last 30 years will continue to be of use in providing snapshots of individual plots of land. However, this approach can never provide a comprehensive understanding of even one site, let alone the history of the entire town. It is like trying to illuminate the whole of Yeovil with matches. Traditional, dirt, archaeology is an expensive and time-consuming process and particularly difficult in an urban environment. Therefore it needs to be employed in conjunction with other, less destructive, methods, many of which have generated material for this book. What is most needed for the future is a programme of planned work, targeted to answer some of the many outstanding questions about Yeovil's hidden history.

CHAPTER 2

PREHISTORY AND THE ROMANS

James Gerrard

INTRODUCTION

Two hundred years ago the age of the earth and humanity was calculated to be a mere 6000 years. The scientific discoveries of the nineteenth and twentieth centuries have revolutionised our understanding of the past. We are now reasonably certain that our earliest ape-like ancestors walked the African plains 3.5 million years ago and that Britain was first inhabited half a million years ago. Of those 500,000 years only 2000 are recorded by historians in written form. Yet the discoveries and innovations that make our modern societies possible developed before the advent of written records. Language, tool making, fire, agriculture, metallurgy, art and religion all began in the prehistoric periods. In Yeovil the periods of the so-called 'Stone Age' are barely represented by surviving sites or finds. There are no stone circles or henges and our knowledge of these remote periods is confined locally to a handful of flint tools. The prehistoric periods are the most obscure of Yeovil's hidden history. It is not until the advent of metallurgy at the beginning of the Bronze Age (around 2000 BC) that we can begin to explore Yeovil's past.

FINDS FROM THE BRONZE AGE

Possibly the most important archaeological find made in the Yeovil area occurred in 1909 on Hendford Hill. A gardener named Henry Cole turned up a gold torc of Middle Bronze Age (1400-1000 BC) date. Torcs are usually seen as being decorative arm or neck rings but this interpretation may not always be valid. Henry Cole's find managed to avoid being melted down surreptitiously for its bullion value (it weighs over 5oz Troy) and after it had been 'cleaned' in battery acid it became the subject of a Treasure Trove inquest. The inquest found that the torc was an isolated find in topsoil brought from three different places in the town and not, therefore Treasure Trove. This enabled the Somerset Archaeological and Natural History Society to purchase the object for £40. It is currently in the collection of the Somerset County Museum in Taunton and replicas are displayed both there and in the Museum of South Somerset in Yeovil.

Gold torcs, indeed any gold artefacts, are exceedingly rare finds even today with metal detecting a common pursuit. Clearly their high intrinsic value meant that they were not lightly discarded in the past. Once they are found, the temptation to turn them into cash has also been a great disincentive for the finder to report them or place them in museum collections. Thus only one other (and very different) gold torc has been found in Somerset, near Ilminster. However, another example similar to the Hendford torc has been found not far from Yeovil at Beer Hackett, near Sherborne and yet another at Ansty, also in Dorset. In fact a study of the known distribution of Bronze Age torcs by George Eogan has shown that they were widely distributed across the British Isles. This tells us little, though, about the societies that produced them and the individuals who wore them.

A starting point for a wider discussion of Bronze Age society is offered by the torc itself. It can be seen as an important, beautiful and prized relic of a long-vanished age. Yet the torc is also an eloquent statement of the skill of the goldsmith who manufactured it. It is made from a sheet of gold 0.04in (1mm) thick and 7.5in (190mm) wide. The sheet was 21.25in (540mm) long. To create the torc a complicated and highly skilled piece of goldsmithing was undertaken (12). The sheet was cut longitudinally into three strips. One of these strips was 0.4in (10mm) wide, the other two 0.18in (4.5mm) wide but the incisions stopped just short of each end of the sheet. The two narrower strips, still attached at each end to the wider strip, were then manipulated so that they stood perpendicular in the centre of each side of the wide strip. Thus in profile the sheet was now cross-shaped. The strips of metal were then soldered together and twisted to produce the classic spiral effect characteristic of torcs. Finally, the two intact pieces of the sheet at either end of the spiral were worked into the hooked terminals.

Before the goldsmiths could begin producing such an impressive item they needed to secure the raw material of their trade: gold. The British Isles were not well endowed with deposits of gold, but it is likely that it came from Ireland. It is possible that Irish gold was exchanged for Cornish tin, a metal vital for alloying with copper to make the harder bronze needed for tools and weapons. Yet even if this argument for bringing the gold to Britain is accepted, another stage is needed to bring the gold to our goldsmith. Whilst it is not known where the Hendford torc was made, it is clear that it was the product

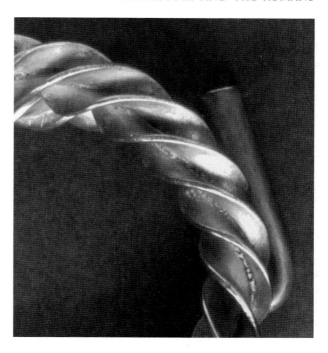

12 Gold torc detail, showing its construction. © *Marjorie Brooke*

of wide exchange networks and highly-developed skills. That all this took place in the Bronze Age proves that it was no primitive and barbaric era. It was a world which, in its own terms, was just as sophisticated as our own.

The Hendford torc stands not only at the pinnacle of Bronze Age goldwork, but also as an expressive statement of the values of the society that produced it. In the period prior to the Bronze Age, known as the Neolithic or New Stone Age, power seems to have been invested in groups of people who might be considered as tribal elders. Their burial rites involved the construction of earthen tombs known as long barrows that were essentially houses for the dead. Their bodies were not buried intact: first they were left to rot and be picked apart by beasts at special mortuary sites (effectively removing the soft tissue). Some time later the surviving bones would be collected up and carefully placed in chambers inside the long barrows. It has been suggested by some archaeologists that this was an attempt to produce a community of the dead in which the individual and individual power had no place. The Early Bronze Age saw the complete transformation of this society.

The reasons for the end of Neolithic social practices are unknown and fiercely debated but it seems likely that metalworking played a significant role in this social transformation. In the Neolithic, the majority of people seem to have had the ability to work stone to produce tools. However, special tools might be manufactured from stones brought from many miles away. Axes produced at Langdale Pike in Cumbria occur all over Britain and in the Somerset Levels an axe made from Alpine jadeite has been recovered. However,

13 Bronze Age axe head found by a metal detector on Wyndham Hill. *With kind permission of the Museum of South Somerset © B. and M. Gittos*

metalworking was a different matter. It involved specialist knowledge that was concentrated in the hands of a few. Just to produce the metal, let alone a useful tool, requires detailed knowledge of which ores to smelt, where to find them and how to cast an object. Furthermore the whole process must have seemed magical to people used to working in stone. Here were metalworkers who could turn stone to liquid and that liquid to a shiny solid and sharp object. One of these Early Bronze Age objects, a so-called 'flat axe' was found by a metal detectorist on Wyndham Hill in Yeovil *(13)*. Since the bronze available was a relatively soft metal, such an axe would not necessarily have been any more useful for cutting trees down than its stone counterpart but its possession must have imbued the user with great social prestige. The individual was becoming important.

Evidence for the importance of the individual in the Early Bronze Age has come from a number of sites around Yeovil. No longer were long earthen barrows constructed to house the dead. Instead people were buried whole, perhaps with grave goods to show their status, under a small and round mound of earth. One of these so-called 'round barrows' was dug in the nineteenth century at Feebarrow (perhaps a corruption of 'three barrows'), near West Coker. Further to the east, near Yeovil Junction railway station, Mr Harbin of Newton Surmaville discovered another Early Bronze Age burial in 1826. This was of a single man, placed in a crouched position in a chamber 3ft wide and 4ft deep. He was accompanied by an intricately decorated pottery drinking vessel and part of a deer's antler *(14)*. The drinking vessel or 'beaker' is a typical find of the period and these pots may, as some analyses have revealed, been associated with another great Bronze Age innovation: the fermentation of honey to produce mead. Close by this grave lay another pit containing a horse skeleton. While it is impossible to say for certain, it is tempting to see the horse as being associated with the human burial. Perhaps it was a sacrifice for the next world.

The Bronze Age burials south of Yeovil and the many similar finds across Britain reinforce the view that the old, communal ways of the Neolithic were being replaced by a new social order, focusing on the individual. The Hendford torc represents this change beautifully. It is an item of jewellery, a thing designed for personal adornment. How it was worn is uncertain but it may never have been used as a neck or arm ring. The diameter of its coils are so small that it would barely fit on the wrist of an adolescent and it is difficult to imagine such a delicate piece of workmanship being coiled and uncoiled to different sizes at will. Thus it may have been made to decorate a child or perhaps as a hair or dress fitting. However, its importance is not in doubt, because the torc represents the highest point of a phenomenon known as the 'ornament horizon'. In the 1950s Margaret Smith studied a number of hoards of Bronze Age metalwork from Somerset. She recognised that in the Middle Bronze Age these hoards began to contain a significant proportion of orna-mental metalwork. This is the 'ornament horizon' which heralded the beginning of widespread embellishment of the body with jewellery. Subsequently, people sought to draw attention to themselves and their impor-tance through lasting objects designed to enhance their personal appearance.

14 Bronze Age beaker and antler fragment found in 1826 associated with a burial at Stoford. *With kind permission of the Somerset County Museum, Taunton © Alan Gittos*

THE ORIGINS OF INDIVIDUAL POWER

By 1200 BC the landscape of today had essentially been created. It was largely deforested and divided by boundaries into units of land and patchworks of fields farmed by small agricultural communities. Then, around 1159 BC, disaster struck. This was the eruption of Mount Hekla, a volcano in Iceland. With Hekla's ash blocking out the sun, the effect would have been something like a nuclear winter. This may have caused a very slight cooling in northern European temperatures which led to climatic deterioration. Areas of upland, like Dartmoor, began to turn to bog and were abandoned. In short, resources were placed under extreme pressure. The Late Bronze Age population's response to this seems to have included warfare. We see large amounts of weaponry, particularly the sword, entering the British archaeological record. By the end of the Bronze Age the status of the individual had changed once more with the formation of a warrior elite and defended hilltop settlements, such as Cadbury Castle, beginning to be constructed.

Through the Iron Age, until the Roman Conquest (in AD 43), the archaeological picture for the Yeovil area is almost blank. This period is represented by only a handful of pottery sherds. This contrasts with the abundance of evidence from the areas to the east and west of the town. It was during the Iron Age that the great hill forts of Cadbury Castle and Ham Hill were at their zenith as centres of population and activity that was virtually 'urban' in its nature. The dearth of evidence from Yeovil is unlikely to be a true reflection of the situation. Instead, it should be regarded as a gap in the current knowledge and understanding of Somerset's past.

ROMAN YEOVIL

At the Roman Conquest in around AD 43-45, the Second Legion, commanded by a man who would become Emperor, marched south and westwards to Isca Dumnoniorum (Exeter) but seem to have made little impact on the Yeovil area. It was a different story at Cadbury and Ham Hill, however, where the great hill forts were stormed and Roman garrisons established within their defences. In the early years following the Conquest, the most significant effect on the local landscape would have been road building. The Roman army constructed an arterial road connecting the fort and, later, town Lindinis (Ilchester) to Durnovaria (Dorchester). This road, still in use as Larkhill Road and the Dorchester Road, presumably aroused some ill feeling among the locals as it undoubtedly cut across the existing field alignments with scant regard for the farmers' thoughts on the matter. A single buckle of Roman military type from West Coker might hint at the troops that would have marched south to Dorchester along this route. However, by the end of the first century all seems to have been quiet in the south west and the troops were moved on. The local population, part of the tribe known as the Durotriges, with their towns at Ilchester and Dorchester, seem to have been happy to accept the opportunities of the Roman Empire.

Westland: one Roman site among many

Many Romano-British sites have been dug in and around Yeovil. Substantial villas and buildings at East and West Coker as well as at Lufton and over the county boundary at Halstock and Bradford Abbas are known. Of these sites, only Lufton and Halstock have been investigated using anything that could be described as modern archaeological field techniques. Space does not permit a detailed description of each site and instead the focus will be on what is, in many ways, the most enigmatic and central Roman site in Yeovil, the Westland villa.

Over the last five years a number of Roman mosaic floors, west of Yeovil at Lopen and Dinnington, have come to light. Yeovil is in the midst of one of the densest concentrations of Roman villas in the country. Yet it is not very well known that at Westland, close to the heart of Yeovil, the Roman site yielded more decorative Roman pavements than Lopen, Dinnington, the two Cokers and Lufton combined. The first hint of what was to be discovered appeared as the slaughter on the Somme came to an end in 1916, when workmen discovered a hoard of Roman coins near Seaton Road. Their importance will be explained later, but here the key point is that this discovery prompted further investigations which uncovered the remains of buildings and a tessellated pavement. As the area was being used for wartime crop production no further investigations were carried out at the site until after the end of the Great War.

Investigation of the Westland site began in earnest after the purchase of the land around it by the Town Council for housing development. Alderman W.R.E. Mitchelmore (1863-1939), an important civic leader and antiquarian after whom Mitchelmore Road is named, led these excavations. By 1926 it was recognised that perhaps the site was beyond the scope of local resources and the Town Council turned to the Society of Antiquaries for advice. Dr (later Sir) Mortimer Wheeler, one of the foremost archaeologists of his generation and excavator of Maiden Castle, Dorset, visited the site and suggested a new plan of action. Three aldermen, including Mitchelmore, formed an excavation committee but the dig itself was to be run by a young associate of Wheeler's, C.A. Raleigh Radford. Radford would become one of the most respected archaeologists of the early medieval period and it was he who identified the Dark Age occupation at Tintagel, Cornwall. However, the young Radford of 1926 was largely untested and untried in the excavation of archaeological sites.

By the standards of his day Radford performed exceptionally well, recording Mitchelmore's finds and extending the excavated area to reveal more traces of buildings. He also published his report within months of completing the work. However by modern, or even the standards of 30 years later, the excavation was a regrettably superficial exercise. Two quotations from Radford's brief report serve to demonstrate this point:

> The work was carried out by means of trial trenches, as the lack of 'finds' did not warrant the expenditure necessary to uncover any large part of the site.

And later,

> Neither the mosaics nor the smaller objects found were of any particular merit... the other finds include only the ordinary articles of Romano-British life, which have been found even in the poor villages of the native peasantry.

Radford apparently saw the Westland site as unexceptional and culturally impoverished. Perhaps more significantly the trial trenches were just narrow excavations, barely two or three spade-widths wide. When a wall or pavement was uncovered, the trench would be expanded to reveal the remains. Thus the excavation technique was heavily biased towards the discovery of substantial stone remains. Timber buildings, which would only survive as the occasional brown stain in the ground, would be well nigh impossible to detect using Mitchelmore's and Radford's excavation techniques. Furthermore the relationship between datable finds such as coins or pottery and the layers they were in was only rarely recorded. This makes establishing dates for many of the buildings on the Westland site extremely difficult. This is harsh criticism of Radford's excavations which were, in reality, typical of their era and better than many conducted by his contemporaries. There were also many mitigating circumstances. He was taking over an investigation which had already been underway for some years and was also restricted by the resources available to him, the aldermen having failed to raise sufficient funds to permit more extensive work. However, a fresh look at the Westland site is clearly justified, in order to try to reinterpret the evidence he recorded.

The Westland site (15) was bounded on two sides by a road constructed of slabs of Yeovil stone overlain by a layer of gravel. It seems probable that these roads connected with the major Roman route from Ilchester to Dorchester described above. The buildings themselves were apparently arranged around a courtyard and formed three blocks. The buildings on the northern side may have served as dwelling spaces while the eastern range was occupied by a bathhouse. On the south side of the courtyard one building with an earth floor may have been a barn while another may also have functioned as living space. Radford saw the Westland site as unremarkable and reading his brief

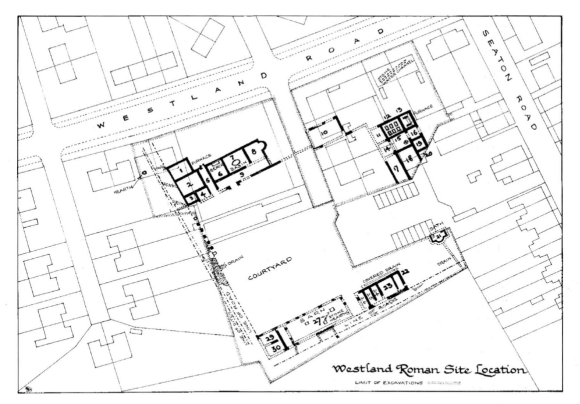

15 Plan of the Westland site shown in relation to the modern street plan. *From a drawing by Leslie Brooke*

description, one could be forgiven for agreeing with him. However, what is remarkable is the number of mosaic pavements on this site. Over half of the rooms were floored with geometric mosaics. This contrasts with the palatial late Roman villa at Woodchester (Gloucestershire) where only approximately one in four rooms in the main building featured mosaics. This makes the Westland site highly unusual and no convincing explanation has ever been given for the large number of mosaics on this site. Most of these mosaics only survived in fragmentary form but the best preserved, found in Room 10, was lifted and placed on display in the Yeovil Museum in King George Street *(16)*. Subsequently, it was transferred to Brympton D'Evercy House, where it still remains, on private property, hidden from public view.

Establishing when the buildings were constructed is extremely difficult. Fortunately Radford noted that pottery was recovered from under buildings in the northern range. The vessels he illustrates are all local products made in the Wareham/Poole Harbour area and are known to archaeologists as Black Burnished ware *(17)*. The vessel form, or shape, suggests that the main period of occupation did not begin until after about AD 250. This fits well with other

16 Roman mosaic from the Westland site when it was being lifted from the floor of the old Museum in King George Street in 1987, ready for its move to Brympton D'Evercy. © *B. and M. Gittos*

17 Black Burnished Romano-British pots from the Westland excavations of the 1920s. Drawn by Sven Schroeder. © *James Gerrard*

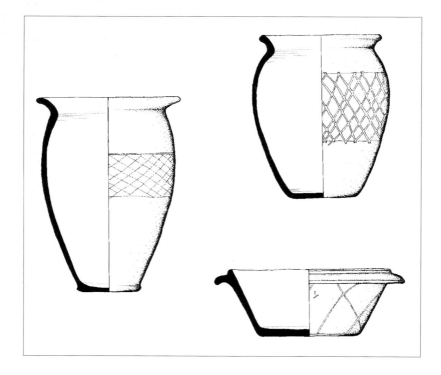

evidence from the site. Only two dozen pieces of the glossy, red Samian tableware of first and second century date was found and, out of 161 coins, only six dated to before AD 238. On this evidence, Radford's suggestion that occupation began around AD 180 would appear to be rather too early and it is more likely that this complex of buildings was, therefore, probably occupied from the late third century onwards.

What can be said of the people who lived in the buildings at Westland and the neighbouring villa sites nearby? We know the names of only two Romano-British Yeovilians. A man at Westland inscribed his name 'MARTINVS' (Martin) on the base of his favourite pottery drinking vessel *(18)* while another, Juventinus Sabinus, dedicated a bronze plaque to the god Mars Rigisamus at West Coker. Mars Rigisamus was a war god and so Sabinus may have had a military connection. In 1949, near a disused quarry off Larkhill Road, a Roman burial was discovered. In the person's mouth was a coin to pay the ferryman (Charon) to take his soul across the River Styx to the Underworld. But what was life like for those who lived at Westland and what did they see when they walked, or rode along the road to Ilchester?

If you were able to fly across Yeovil in the year AD 300 you would see a landscape not unfamiliar. There is a major road running south to Dorchester and it is visible as a broad stripe, straight as an arrow cutting across this agricultural scene. Minor roads and tracks feed the main road and these serve the patchwork of fields with their crops of wheat, barley and beans. Small stands of woodland exist, heavily managed and exploited for timber, fuel and as foraging land for pigs. The wetland along the river and stream banks is largely under pasture and grazed by small cattle, kept mainly for their dairying potential. The hillsides would be dotted with sheep although their wool would probably be brown and not white. People are very visible in this landscape. About every

18 Base of a Roman pottery beaker with the name 'MARTINVS' scratched on it. From the Westland site and now in the collection of the Museum of South Somerset. © *B and M Gittos*

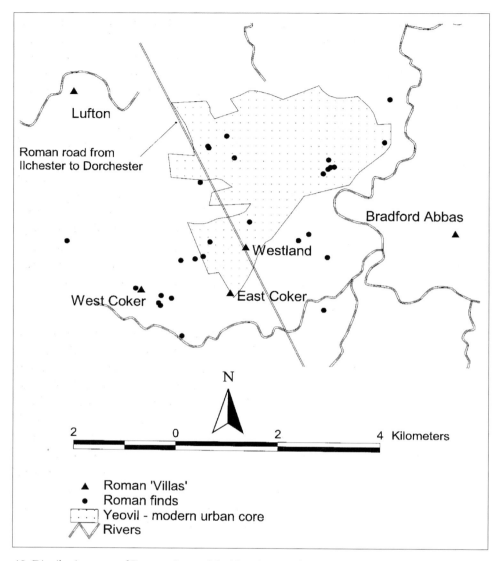

19 Distribution map of Roman sites and find locations in the Yeovil area. © *James Gerrard*

kilometre a small group of farm buildings cluster together. They are largely made of wood, although occasionally a small rectangular stone building might be visible. The occupants of these settlements will be busy tending the crops and moving the cattle along the trackways from pasture to byre. To one side of the road stand the stone buildings of Westland and the smoke from the furnace heating water for the bathhouse hangs grey in the air. Further south, where the road from Ilchester climbs to the higher land of Coker, there are two more substantial groups of buildings, the villas of East and West Coker. The buildings here are large masonry structures roofed with stone slates or red clay tiles. The owners of the East Coker villa might be out hunting in the woods. They seem to have enjoyed hunting, since a fine mosaic pavement from the site depicts two men bringing home a slain stag *(colour plate 2)*. It is to these estate centres and their owners that many of the local farmers will owe a portion of their produce at harvest time.

It is a sleepy, rural scene and the evidence for it is drawn not only from finds in the town but also elsewhere in Somerset. Recent work at Yeovilton and around South Cadbury has shown that every serviceable piece of land was being used for farming. Many modern field boundaries have their origins in the Roman period in this part of the country. Romano-British farmsteads are known from sites near Somerton like Bradley Hill and Catsgore (see Chapter 1). One has yet to be excavated in Yeovil but, for instance, finds of pottery from Westfield Avenue, St Michael's Avenue and Pen Mill point to their existence. The map *(19)* shows the distribution of Roman finds in the area and their density suggests that many other sites are covered by the modern town.

A Milestone and an Emperor

Sleepy and rural the picture may have been but the inhabitants of the villas were not backwoods rustics isolated from the Roman world. Occasionally events that would shake the Empire and change the course of history would stretch their tentacles into the south west, as a find from the parish of Stoke sub Hamdon reveals. To the west of Yeovil, the A303 follows the course of the Fosse Way, the great Roman road from Exeter to Lincoln. It crosses Trutt's Brook at the site of the now-demolished Venn Bridge (near the Cartgate roundabout). In 1930, workmen widening the road at this point found a column of limestone with mouldings at its base *(20)*. Close inspection revealed that the original surface had been roughly chiselled away and a new inscription had been carved on it. Although this column began its life as part of a very well-appointed building, it had been reused at a later date as a milestone. The inscription, which is crudely cut, reads:

IMPFLVAL
SEVEROPI
OFELNOB
CAES

This can be translated as 'For the Emperor Flavius Valerius Severus, pious and fortunate, most noble Caesar'. Flavius Valerius Severus ruled for only a brief period, from AD 305 to 307 and was one of the great unfulfilled hopes of the early fourth century. The third century had been a period of crisis for the Empire. It was riven by civil and external warfare and economic problems. At the end of the third century a soldier named Diocletian became Emperor. In

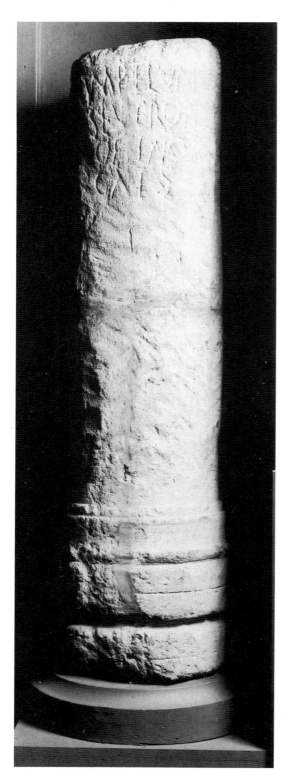

20 Left Roman milestone, commemorating the Emperor Flavius Valerius Severus, AD 305–307, discovered during road widening in 1930 on the course of the Fosse Way near the Venn Bridge. Now on display in the Somerset County Museum Taunton. © *Alan Gittos*

21 Above A coin of Constantine I (AD 307–324), minted in London. None were found in the Westland hoard but the same issue was in the mouth of the Larkhill burial. © *B. and M. Gittos*

an attempt to avoid civil war and make imperial power more effective, Diocletian adopted a political system that has become known as the tetrarchy, or rule of four. Under this complicated and ultimately unworkable system the Empire was divided into an eastern and western half. Each half had a Senior Emperor or Augustus. Under the Augusti were an eastern and western Caesar. Each Caesar would expect to become Augustus on the death or abdication of his senior colleague.

On 1 May AD 305 the Empire was ruled by the four successors of Diocletian. In the east Galerius was Augustus and his junior colleague was the Caesar Maximinus. In the west the Augustus was Constantius Chlorus and the Caesar was a soldier described by one source as middle-aged, violent, and hard drinking (although this could apply to almost any late Roman Emperor!). This Caesar was the Severus recorded on the milestone. Severus directly ruled Africa and Italy. So why is he commemorated on a Somerset milestone, especially as there is only one other stone in Britain bearing his name?

In AD 305 the senior Emperor in the west, Constantius Chlorus, was in Britain campaigning against the Picts north of Hadrian's Wall. His 35-year-old son, Constantine, was with him and the Augustus was ill, very ill. He died the following year, at Eboracum (York). Severus automatically succeeded him as Augustus and it was down to Severus to select his junior colleague. However, Constantine was popular with his father's army and pre-empted Severus' decision. On 25 July AD 306 Constantine was illegally proclaimed Augustus by the troops based at Eboracum. In an attempt to avoid civil war, Constantine was recognised as Caesar but by late October another usurper named Maxentius had been proclaimed Augustus in Rome. When Severus marched against Maxentius, his army deserted him and he surrendered on the understanding that his life would be spared. This was not to be and Severus perished.

Severus was a friend and political ally of the Augustus in the east, Galerius. The milestone at Venn Bridge may, therefore, have been an attempt to remind the wealthy, and presumably politically astute, population of Roman Somerset who the legitimate successor to the popular (at least in Britain) Constantius would be. It is equally significant that once Constantine had been proclaimed Emperor, milestones were set up bearing his name to remind the traveller that not only was he the Emperor but also the son of Constantius. It was his blood and his army that made Constantine Emperor, not the law of succession laid down by Diocletian.

History is written by the victors, and Constantine was to emerge as sole Emperor of the Roman world in AD 324 *(21)*. His dynasty was to rule the Empire for another 40 years. Constantine (the Great) also became the first Christian Emperor and his new religion spread quickly due to his influence. Mosaics with Christian iconography have been found at Hinton St Mary, east of Yeovil near Sturminster Newton, and at Frampton in Dorset. Constantine was a man who changed the world. In contrast, the reign and political importance of Severus are only hinted at in Britain by a few lines roughly incised on a stone from Venn Bridge and preserved in the County Museum, Taunton.

Buried treasure

Coincidentally Constantine and his dynasty feature heavily in what is perhaps Yeovil's most significant discovery of the Roman period. This was not a mosaic, nor walls nor even pottery. The finder was a workman laying a water main to supply the Westland Aircraft Factory in 1916 and the discovery was over 800 Roman bronze coins. Most of these coins rapidly found their way into the hands of the workman's friends, colleagues and a local businessman called Edgar Vincent. In short, this hoard nearly vanished without a trace. Fortunately a man who has been described as 'the father of Somerset archaeology' received word of what had happened. Harold St George Gray was a student of General Augustus Lane-Fox Pitt Rivers, a man who can justifiably be described as the 'father of modern British archaeology'. What separated Pitt Rivers from many other late nineteenth-century archaeologists and antiquarians was his obsession with detailed recording of his excavations and finds. To Pitt Rivers the smallest piece of pottery was as important as a gold coin. He also owned most of Cranborne Chase in Dorset and so had plenty of opportunity to investigate archaeological sites on his own land. From Pitt Rivers, St George Gray learnt his archaeological skills and the importance of keeping detailed records. He excavated at many local sites near Yeovil including Cadbury Castle, Ham Hill and the Glastonbury Lake villages. In fact so good was his record-keeping that parts of the latter site could be written up and published by John Coles of Exeter University 20 years after St George Gray's death. He examined, with characteristic thoroughness, all the coins from the Yeovil hoard that he could locate – some 852 specimens. He estimated that originally over 1,000 had been present in the ground. This would make the hoard one of the largest late Roman bronze coin hoards in the country. The results of St George Gray's study, with his coin identifications, were published in the county archaeological journal and his article remains the sole record of this very important discovery.

The Westland hoard, as St George Gray's records reveal, comprised coins solely of the house of Constantine. As described above, Constantine is remembered as the first Christian Roman Emperor. However, some coins from the Westland hoard bear the legend DIVUS CONSTANTINUS (the divine Constantine) a reminder that his sons deified him as a god on his death in AD 337. The latest coin in the Westland hoard is of Constantine's son Constantius II who died in AD 361. There is no record of any coins minted after this date so it seems likely that the hoard was deposited in the early AD 360s, perhaps during the reign of the Emperor Julian (AD 361-363). St George Gray offered no explanation for the hoard, other than suggesting that it was likely to have been concealed deliberately. However, Raleigh Radford had a very definite explanation for this find, in his account of the Westland site:

> ...disaster overtook the rural dwellings about 370AD. The historical reason for this end is known... the year 367 saw a double disaster to the Roman armies in the province. Geographically Somerset lies open to invaders from Ireland, and even though there was no actual sack of the settlements the burial of the Yeovil hoard... reflects the growing sense of insecurity. Threatened by these raiders, the more wealthy inhabitants preferred the shelter of walled towns... and left their country houses, doubtless cherishing the vain hope of an eventual return when the troubled period should have passed.

This brief and evocative account of the end of the Westland site sees the coin hoard as a symptom of political and military insecurity. In AD 367 the Roman historian Ammianus Marcellinus records that the Picts (in what is now Scotland), the Scots (from Ireland) and the Saxons made an alliance known as the barbarian conspiracy and attacked Roman Britain. As barbarians overran the province wealthy civilians fled and took shelter until fresh troops arrived to restore order. Some of those civilians were unable to weather this storm and were thus unable to return and collect their hidden riches.

The barbarian conspiracy is a neat explanation for the abandonment of the Westland, and many other sites. Unfortunately, this theory is not supported by the evidence. The man who commanded the troops that restored Britain to the Empire in the wake of the so-called barbarian conspiracy was none other than the father of Theodosius the Great, the Emperor at the time Ammianus was writing. Consequently, it seems likely that Ammianus exaggerated the whole incident to please the Emperor. Furthermore, there is virtually no archaeological evidence that this event took place. There are no villas clearly destroyed by fire in AD 367 and nothing to indicate the destruction of towns or forts along Hadrian's Wall. The Westland hoard was probably buried several years too early to be connected with this event, so why was it concealed? Many large hoards of late Roman bronze coinage have been found in Somerset and southern England. Perhaps, as Radford suggested, these might have been a response to insecurity and barbarian raiding. Maybe the Westland hoard was buried by the victim of an otherwise unrecorded incident. Alternatively, the person who buried it might have died without telling his relatives, or simply forgotten exactly where he had buried his life savings. All of these suggestions are possible but another explanation is much more compelling.

Late Roman coinage was essentially made out of either precious (gold or silver) or non-precious (bronze) metal. The bronze coinage was overvalued in relation to the market price of its metal content. In short, its purchasing power was greater than its scrap metal value. It was, therefore, only acceptable as coinage so long as it could be exchanged for gold or silver. Even today a paper banknote, itself valueless, bears a promise from the Bank of England to pay the bearer its value in coin. Thus a hoard of bronze coins, with little scrap value, would become worthless if the Roman state no longer agreed to exchange them for gold or silver coinage. In this unfortunate situation there would be no point in spending time recovering worthless savings. This is the most likely reason for the owner abandoning the Westland hoard. It can be demonstrated by comparing the range of coins it contained with that of later bronze hoards found locally and others from a series of signal stations built on the Yorkshire coast after around AD 370. This information is summarised in the table.

	WESTLAND	WEYMOUTH	WIVELISCOMBE	SIGNAL STATIONS
Pre-Constantinian	0	34	10	2
Constantine (AD 306–337)	110	51	17	3
House of Constantine (AD 337–363)	733	286	108	15
House of Valentinian (AD 364–378)	0	389	866	86
House of Theodosius (AD 378–402)	0	3512	55	29
Unidentifiable	9	0	83	0
TOTAL	852	4272	1139	235

The Weymouth (Dorset) and Wiveliscombe (Somerset) hoards are both larger than what remained from the Westland hoard and must have been concealed after about AD 388 which is the date of their latest coins. The Yorkshire signal stations were probably built after about AD 370. Thus, the coins lost at those sites reflect the coins in use by their occupants in the last two or three decades of the fourth century. What is striking is that in the Weymouth and Wiveliscombe hoards and at the signal stations, Constantinian and earlier coins are relatively rare, accounting for less than one in ten of the total. The Westland hoard was probably buried during the politically difficult reign of Julian, when civil and external war threatened the Empire. The lack of coins of that Emperor is understandable as they are relatively rare in Britain. When Valentinian I became Emperor a new, smaller coinage was issued and we can suggest that Constantinian issues were largely demonetised. Thus they occur rarely in later hoards and the owner of the Westland coins did not return to collect them, as they were now largely valueless.

The end of Roman Yeovil
The end of the Roman Empire is a very controversial issue. Radford believed that Westland was abandoned due to the fear of raiders and invaders. However, the archaeological evidence does not support the idea of a violent end to Roman Yeovil. So what did happen?

On the last day of December AD 406 barbarians crossed the frozen Rhine and raided deep into Gaul. The troops in Britain, and no doubt the wealthy villa owners, feared isolation from the continent. Consequently they proclaimed Constantine III Emperor, as they had done a century earlier with his namesake, Constantine the Great. Constantine III took most of his army to Gaul in an attempt to defeat the barbarians. Ultimately he was to fail and he met his fate at the hands of soldiers loyal to the legitimate Emperor Honorius. In AD 410 Honorius wrote a letter to what is usually said to be the cities of Britain telling them 'to look to their own defence'. This letter may actually refer to the cities of Bruttium in southern Italy. Whether this does refer to Britain is ultimately academic since after Constantine III's departure Britain went its own way, lost to the Empire by default.

In Somerset and across most of the country the early fifth century is a shadowy time difficult to identify, excavate and make sense of archaeologically. At the Lufton villa in the late fourth or early fifth century the fine mosaic pavements become covered with domestic refuse: pottery, bone, charcoal and oyster shells. In one room a furnace for iron smithing was dug into a mosaic. Some archaeologists interpret this as evidence of a decline in standards. The civilisation of the fourth century had sunk to primitive barbarism in the fifth. However, this is probably the wrong way to look at evidence like that found at Lufton. A villa was a nice place to live, but also made a prime target in lawless times. More importantly, in the fifth century the need to use available buildings for economically productive activities, like metalworking, might have been very pressing. The early fifth century was a period of change. The great landowners were probably transforming themselves into warlords with their own bands of warriors in these new and unstable times. These local warlords would have looked back to Rome and seen themselves as descendants and successors of that Empire. They were Christian and some of them probably read Latin and used Roman military titles. Undoubtedly, they fought against their neighbours and, later, the people in the east of the country who would become known as the Anglo-Saxons. The most successful of these warlords seem to have been emerging as kings by the end of the fifth century. About AD 470 the great hill fort at Cadbury Castle was re-fortified. The people who lived within its defences traded with what was left of the Roman Empire around Constantinople in the Eastern Mediterranean. For the ordinary folk the rhythm of agricultural life, of planting, harvesting and paying tribute to their lord went on largely unchanged by the fall of the Roman Empire.

In the early seventh century, high up on the ridge overlooking the now abandoned Cadbury Castle, at least six people were buried. Some were interred with metalwork and weaponry like that used in the pagan Anglo-Saxon areas to the east. When these burials were excavated it was thought that they might be Anglo-Saxon migrants moving into Somerset, conquering it from the Britons. A scientific analysis of two of these burials (excavated by Bristol

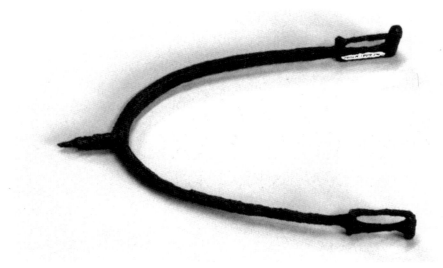

22 Late Saxon spur found during the excavations at Westland in the 1920s. *With kind permission of the Museum of South Somerset. © B. and M. Gittos*

University in 2001) revealed that both had been brought up very locally. It seems that 2000 years ago the people of what is today Somerset chose to be Roman. One thousand four hundred years ago they chose to be Anglo–Saxon. Yet the shadow of Rome was, and is, a long one. A spur, probably of tenth-century date, was found by Radford at Westland, although not mentioned in his report *(22)*. This is one of the few pieces of late Saxon material from the town. How it came to be on a site that had probably been abandoned for five centuries is a matter for guesswork. Perhaps the person who lost it was looking and marvelling at the ruins of Roman Yeovil.

CHAPTER 3

YEOVIL'S ANGLO-SAXON MINSTER

Brian and Moira Gittos

MINSTER CHURCHES

One of the most attractive aspects of the town of Yeovil is the prominent and fine fourteenth-century parish church of St John the Baptist *(colour plate 1)*. Yet there is compelling evidence that, in its place, Yeovil was once focused around an Anglo-Saxon minster church and that this lost building provided the nucleus from which grew the town we see today. Minsters had a special role in the hierarchy of Anglo-Saxon churches. They were effectively the senior church for a given area, acting as a mother church for a group of neighbouring, dependent 'daughter' chapels. The minsters presided over parishes (*parochiae*), which were large units encompassing the territory of the dependent parishes and possibly reflecting earlier land usage such as Roman and pre-Roman estates. Insufficient records survive to identify churches as former minsters but in addition to former daughter churches, other good indicators are proximity to a royal manor and the role of the settlement as the centre of a pre-Conquest area of local administration known as the hundred. As will become clear, Yeovil can lay claim to all three attributes.

Detailed studies of particular parts of England such as Hampshire and south-east Shropshire have demonstrated how, in the Middle Saxon period, the landscape was divided from an ecclesiastical point of view, into a network of large parishes controlled by minster churches. The ancient rights of the minster church, over the sacraments of baptism and burial, were jealously guarded. This was because they provided a major economic advantage, derived from charges and taxes, for what were essential services in the medieval world. A prime example of this was the levy termed 'soulscot', which was payable to the minster by virtue of its right of burial. It is a payment of this kind which provides the first clue to the existence of such a church at Yeovil.

HISTORICAL BACKGROUND

Yeovil is fortunate in being mentioned in two important Anglo-Saxon documents. The first is the will of a lady named Wynflaed. She was possibly a member of the royal house but was certainly a person of some consequence in mid-tenth century England, holding extensive property in the southern counties. Wynflaed makes it clear that half a pound's worth of soulscot should be rendered to Yeovil (written as *Gifle)*, from her estate at Chinnock. She was concerned that things should be done properly after her death, stressing that sufficient be provided from Chinnock because soulscot *must* be rendered from that manor to Yeovil. A payment was also due from her estate at Charlton Horethorne to Milborne Port, another minster church with a *parochia* to the east of Sherborne. As well as demonstrating Yeovil's status as a potential minster, Wynflaed's will also suggests that any church at Chinnock was subservient to Yeovil, lacking burial rights of its own. More recent references indicate that other chapels and churches also acted as daughter churches to Yeovil. As late as the eighteenth century, areas of St John's churchyard were segregated for burials from Kingston and Yeovil Marsh, where there were chapels with no right of burial. Other dependant churches and chapels noted by Bob Dunning are Barwick, Brympton, Chilton Cantelo, Mudford, Preston, Sock Dennis and Tintinhull. However, the earliest record which has relevance to understanding Yeovil's early church is the will of King Alfred, who died in AD 899. In the will, land in Yeovil is mentioned as one of seven royal possessions in Somerset. There is no mention of a church but the usefulness of this evidence is its confirmation that Yeovil had another of the likely indicators for the presence of a minster church, the proximity of a royal manor. This is almost certainly what has become enshrined in the place name 'Kingston', the northernmost of the two Yeovil manors.

Yeovil's role as the centre of a hundred is well attested in the historical record. Originally a Saxon land unit used for administrative and legal purposes (for example, the hundred courts provided the evidence for the Domesday Survey Commissioners), the division of counties into hundreds dates from the tenth century and was still utilised in the nineteenth. It was even chosen as the vehicle for arranging the Victoria County Histories of England (still in progress today). Often a hundred was named according to the chief town in the locality such as the hundreds of Crewkerne and South Petherton. This was not so for Yeovil, where it had the intriguing title of the Hundred of Stone. This almost certainly referred to a local landmark, the Hundred Stone at the junction of Combe Street Lane, Mudford Road and Stone Lane *(23)*. This was the hundred meeting place, where the moot was held. The last recorded meeting was in 1843, when a libation was poured into the hole in the top of the stone before the assembly adjourned to the Three Choughs for refreshments. It is possible that the use of the non-specific term 'Stone' for the hundred name derives from special significance attached to this landmark.

23 The Hundred Stone at the junction of Mudford Road and Stone Lane, the meeting place of the Hundred of Stone from Anglo-Saxon times. © *B. and M. Gittos*

The Domesday Book is silent on the subject of a church at Yeovil. This is not surprising since, amongst the 611 land holdings listed in Somerset, only 17 churches are mentioned and in Dorset, none at the suggestively named Beaminster, Charminster, Iwerne Minster, Lychett Minster, Sturminster or Yetminster. Yeovil's case is not, therefore, weakened by this omission. The Domesday record does, however, containing an intriguing reference to an independent joint holding by 22 men of 22 plots of land. There has been much debate about the significance of this arrangement but it seems likely that it describes the nucleus of what was subsequently called 'the tenement' and which grew into the medieval town.

In 1219, in the church of St Mary Major, Ilchester, the king's justices made a judgement on a dispute between Walerand, parson of the church of Yeovil, and Sir John Maltravers, lord of the manor of Hendford. The verdict given confirmed that the rents and income from the tenement of Yeovil were to be placed on the altar of St John's, for the sole benefit of the church. It also confirmed that the parson of the church was effectively lord over the holders of the tenement and had the right to hold courts. This describes an unusual situation, in which the incumbent of the church of Yeovil was also lord of the town, a conflict of interest which created controversy until the fifteenth century. However, it is the detail of this document which is most helpful in relation to Yeovil's early church. It states that the rights confirmed by the judgement had originally been conferred by the 'daughter of a certain king'. It has been suggested that this reference is to the Empress Mathilda, in the twelfth century. However, what seems more likely is that it refers to events which occurred before the Norman Conquest and the names of the royalty involved were no longer recalled. Dunning has made further observations concerning the clerical jurors, suggesting that they had been carefully selected because of their knowledge of Yeovil's church. He points out for example, that three of them were chaplains of probable daughter churches at Brympton, Chilton (Cantelo) and Mudford. The 1219 judgement is also useful in that it provides early confirmation that the church was dedicated to St John the Baptist. This is reflected in the town seals, which in the fourteenth century had a strongly religious flavour, bearing a representation of the *Agnus Dei* (Lamb of God, the symbol of St John the Baptist) and carrying the legend '*Sigill Sancti Johannis Baptiste*' (Seal of Saint John the Baptist). The identity of the town is being inextricably linked with the church and all subsequent town seals have carried such symbolism. A few years later, in 1226, Richard de Say gave land in Yeovil to the Priory of Montacute, in a charter made 'in the Great Church' of Yeovil. This description, omitted from the abbreviated published version of the Montacute Cartulary (the monastery's record of its land grants), is particularly significant in the light of events which were to unfold during the next century.

By the fourteenth-century references to St John's become more numerous. Two registers survive from the bishops of Bath and Wells, those of John Droxford (1309-29) and Ralph of Shrewsbury (1329-63). From them, the names and activities of some of the rectors and vicars of Yeovil can be recovered. In medieval Yeovil, the incumbent of St John's was the rector, who employed a vicar to carry out his pastoral duties. The registers also mention disputes between the rectors and the town burgesses, arising out of the former's dual role as lord of the town and parson of the parish church. It is reasonable to assume that it was this continuing tension which was the root cause of the dramatic events of 1349. Bishop Ralph of Shrewsbury was conducting a formal visitation (an inspection of the way in which the clergy and parish conducted themselves) when his retinue was attacked by a mob of townsfolk, led by Roger Warmwille of Newton Surmaville. The miscreants were armed with bows, arrows, iron bars, stones and other weapons. Mayhem ensued, with the bishop and his servants being imprisoned in the church until nightfall. They were subsequently moved to the rectory before being rescued by neighbours the following day. The cause of the riot is not recorded and we are left to surmise that such was the depth of feeling between the religious and the secular in Yeovil, that the bishop (the most senior churchman the townsfolk were likely to encounter) was targeted in order to vent their anger at the highest level. Punishment followed, with excommunication for the rioters, and Yeovil and its dependent churches being placed under interdict (a prohibition on the administration of the sacraments and holding of religious services, including burial of the dead). The lengthy descriptions of the events themselves and the penances imposed yield one small piece of information about the church itself. As part of their penance, the malefactors were required to '... stand on Sundays on a lofty place of the said church bare headed etc whilst the divine offices are being celebrated...'. The use of the term 'lofty place' could imply the top of a tower or an external parapet but the point of the exercise was that the penitents should be on public view during the service, making it much more likely that an internal 'lofty place' was intended. It may be no coincidence that this is a concept especially appropriate to a pre-Conquest building. Pre-Conquest churches were often provided with spaces on high, visible from the body of the church, in the form of high-level doorways or galleries. Another important point arising out of the 1349 debacle is the fact that the churchyard was considered to have been polluted by the spilling of human blood. This desecration may have had far reaching consequences.

In 1362, John de Risingden's long tenure of the rectorship came to an end when Bishop Ralph permitted an exchange of benefices between the rectors of Yeovil and Merriot. By this means Robert de Sambourne became rector and, some time during the next 20 years, he began work on a completely new church in the Perpendicular style. The architect may well have been William Wynford who was the master mason at Wells and Winchester Cathedrals and, through his work for Bishop William of Wykham, was also involved in the building of Winchester College and New College, Oxford. Wynford and Sambourne gave Yeovil the parish church we know today, its structure remaining substantially unchanged after 600 years. The evidence that Sambourne was responsible for the work is contained in his will, which instructs his executors to devote his estate, foremost, to the work of the church of Yeovil 'begun by me' 'until it is finished'. It has been suggested that the desecration of 1349 provided the spur for rebuilding the church. However, the delay of perhaps more than 20 years suggests that there may have been other strong reasons for the drastic action of demolishing the old church and starting anew. Many churches had substantial work carried out during the medieval period, often by successive generations, but the total rebuilding of a church, such as at Yeovil, occurred less frequently.

This decision to rebuild has to be seen against the background of the 1226 description of the 'Great Church' of Yeovil. If the earlier church had been 'great' because of its status rather than its stature, perhaps by the later fourteenth century (150 years later) it was outdated and inadequate for the liturgical needs of Sambourne, who was both a wealthy patron and canon of Wells. It is possible that it was the Anglo-Saxon minster church in which the bishop was imprisoned in 1349 and which was swept away in the rebuilding. There is circumstantial evidence to support this hypothesis. If there had been a twelfth-century rebuilding of the pre-Conquest church, it would have had architectural details (such as doorways or arches) decorated with Romanesque carving but no fragments of this character have ever been found in Yeovil. If the pre-Conquest church had been upgraded in the thirteenth century, the building would still have been relatively new and probably in good repair. It is very unlikely that Sambourne would have considered it worthwhile to devote so much money to its total replacement. Similarly, no thirteenth-century elements have ever been discovered and, in an age when stone was too valuable a commodity ever to be discarded, this absence is significant.

Archpriest

Sambourne's interest in St John's was manifest long before he became rector. In the late 1340s, he had founded a chantry dedicated to the Holy Trinity in the old church and it had been richly endowed. One unusual feature of this act of piety was the way in which the chantry was organised. The endowments were to pay for the services of two chaplains, who were to be overseen by an arch-priest. This was an uncommon appointment in the middle of the fourteenth century but two examples are known from Devon. In the previous decade, similar arrangements had been made at Beer Ferrers (1335) and at Haccombe (1334). In both cases, the archpriest was the senior member of a small group of chantry priests and curiously in both cases the incumbent still bears this title today. At St Martin le Grand, Dover, an archpriest officiated until 1536. In this case, instead of being an official associated with a chantry foundation, it seems likely that the office was a survival of a role which had had greater significance in the Anglo-Saxon period. Mother churches were not usually monasteries in the modern sense of the term but were staffed by a small community of priests overseen by a head priest or archpriest. This arrangement was widely used throughout the Christian world and archpriest is still an office and title within the Orthodox churches. Whether Yeovil's minster operated in this way is a matter of conjecture but it is conceivable that knowledge of such a title had lingered in the town in the fourteenth century and its revival might have appealed to a cleric such as Sambourne. The adoption of this archaic termi-nology could have been a method of reasserting the historic importance of the parish church, which was to be such a focus for Sambourne's energy and resources throughout the rest of the century. Whatever the reason, the appointment of an archpriest of Holy Trinity chantry continued well into the fifteenth century and an impression of a seal of the archpriest has survived. The archpriest at Beer Ferrers enjoyed a number of privileges, which included exemption from diocesan jurisdiction and he was responsible directly to the archbishop of Canterbury. Consequently, in procession he was positioned alongside the diocesan bishop and in the sanctuary of the church, his seat was placed on the same side as the bishop's. Whether Yeovil's archpriest was similarly empowered is not recorded but in any event he was not the rector.

THE SEARCH FOR THE MINSTER CHURCH OF YEOVIL

The best place to open the search is with the present building. Can it tell us anything about its predecessor? The present church is a remarkably coherent design which seems to have been constructed in a single campaign over, perhaps, 20 years. The only part of the church which is of a different date is the crypt which appears to be a little earlier and this is particularly true of the elaborate doorway on the north side of the chancel, at the top of the staircase leading to it. The carving on this doorway is in the Decorated style, the type of architecture which preceded the Perpendicular (in which the rest of the building is designed). The Decorated elements point to a start having been made on the new church at the eastern end of the building. When radical rebuilding was planned, work often started at the east end, to ensure that it was the liturgically important chancel which was ready for use first. However, in the case of Yeovil, other considerations may also have influenced this decision and, furthermore, John Harvey has suggested for St John's a plausible variation on the east–west building sequence. He argues that it would have been prudent to begin building such a large tower at an early stage to avoid separation from the nave due to preferential settlement of the heavier structure. Therefore, work would have started first on the tower, chancel and transepts, with the nave completed as the final stage.

One striking feature of the present building is its location, on the very edge of a sharp change of level, above Silver Street. The end of the chancel is extremely close to the drop but the land also slopes down towards this point, the highest ground being at the west end. The string courses on the outside of the church demonstrate the effect clearly (24). The change in height created a problem for the architect, since in order to maintain a level floor from west to east it was necessary for the chancel to be raised. A clever solution to this problem was the inclusion in the design of a room below the chancel which would serve the purpose of supporting the sanctuary at the desired level and also provide additional accommodation. Given this arrangement, it is not surprising that it was this supporting structure which was built first. Since the room is largely above ground it should, perhaps, not be termed a crypt and possible uses

include a meeting place for the clergy, a vestry or a chapel. If there had been a strong liturgical need for the provision of a crypt at Yeovil, the same would have been the case for many other parish churches and clearly this did not happen. There is, however, an interesting comparison at Madley in Herefordshire, where, early in the fourteenth century, a large chancel was added to an existing building over ground which sloped away to the east. A two-level structure was created with a room beneath the chancel which, like Yeovil, was stone vaulted with a central octagonal pier. It differs from Yeovil in being larger and having a different moulding for the vault ribs but the principle is the same.

As we have seen, the siting of the church gave the architect a structural problem in providing a level floor through the church and this raises a question as to why it was necessary (or desirable) to position the new building in such a difficult location, rather than elsewhere in the churchyard. The structure provides another pointer to the presence of constraints in laying out the building. The windows of the nave are of a consistent design and size. They must have been made to a single, standardised, drawing and are intended to fill the entire wall space, between the structural uprights. However, on both north and south walls, it has been necessary to recess one window behind the corner of the transept in order to permit the design to fit *(25)*. This supports the suggestion made earlier that the nave was completed after the tower, chancel

24 Opposite East end of the chancel, St John's church. The string courses demonstrate the slope of the ground. © *B. and M. Gittos*

25 Right Window recessed into the wall of the transept. North side of nave, St John's church. © *B. and M. Gittos*

and transepts. Only at the end of the building sequence might it have been appreciated that there was insufficient space for the size of the nave windows. Why was the space for building the new church at such a premium? Two possibilities present themselves. Either the new church was built around the old church (although larger and occupying more space) or, as seems more likely, the space was simply not available, since the old church and, perhaps, associated buildings were still standing, immediately to the west.

The next piece of the jigsaw concerns the Schoolhouse or Chantry. This is the building which now stands, albeit in nineteenth-century guise, to the west of the churchyard *(26)*. It was erected as we see it today, after the old building had been taken down, in 1855, to provide more space in the churchyard. The old building had stood adjoining the church tower, as is shown in several early illustrations *(27)*. It had not always been a school, having been purchased by the parish for that purpose in 1576. Previously, it had been a chantry chapel dedicated to St Mary the Virgin. Early documents refer to it as the chantry in the churchyard, to distinguish it from the four other chantries located within the church, one of which was also dedicated to the Blessed Virgin. In this respect there is an interesting comparison with the minster church at Crewkerne, which also had a separate chantry in the churchyard, dedicated to Our Lady. This was founded in 1309 by Agnes de Monceaux and dissolved in

26 Left The Chantry, as rebuilt in 1855. © *B. and M. Gittos*

27 Opposite The Chantry abutting the tower of St John's, prior to its rebuilding on the new site. The Engine House fills the gap between it and the end of the south aisle. Drawing by Leslie Brooke, after *Gentleman's Magazine*, 1824. © *Marjorie Brooke*

1548, probably being demolished soon after to recover the value of the lead roof (£6 13s 4d). Its precise location is unknown.

John Leland visited Yeovil in the 1540s, whilst touring the country to record antiquities on behalf of King Henry VIII. He made special mention of this chapel, which evidently puzzled him and he said that 'it seemith more ancient than the paroche', i.e. the parish church. Leland was a man with considerable experience of examining churches and other buildings and his judgement in this case is likely to have been well founded. The chantry chapel was, indeed, an older building and, curiously, it was not part of the main structure but lay with its north-east corner in the angle between the south-west buttresses of the tower, corner to corner with the church. In the early nineteenth century, the space between its east end and the end of the south aisle had been filled by a short-lived lean-to known as the Engine House (visible in *27*), used to accommodate the town's fire engine. However, the important point is that the chantry in the churchyard and Robert Sambourne's church, although extremely close together (possibly even touching), were separate buildings.

Attention now switches to the Chantry chapel itself. Unfortunately, the usual description, of it being 'moved' to a new site, creates something of a misapprehension. The truth is that it was demolished and totally rebuilt, retaining a few of its original features. Most of the building as it stands dates from 1855, including the doorways and a complete set of new windows. The retained items comprise a piscina *(28)*, two image niches and a set of corbel heads supporting the roof timbers (these allegedly copied from the original roof). The most telling detail is the piscina, with its sweeping ogee form which clearly dates it to the first half of the fourteenth century. It has two shields above the arch which, although they have lost their painted heraldry, provide the clue that the person or family responsible for the chantry bore arms. The style of the piscina suggests that the chapel was built just prior to the Black Death and was therefore still a relatively new building when Sambourne's church was erected. This is corroborated by the fact that during demolition of the chapel, a fine thirteenth-century cross head (probably from a churchyard cross) was found built into the wall. It is now preserved in the Roman Catholic church.

28 Fourteenth-century piscina in the south wall of the rebuilt Chantry.
© *B. and M. Gittos*

If the family who created the chantry were still in the area, they were likely to have been vocal in opposing its demolition.

Some useful information appeared in the *Western Flying Post, Sherborne Mercury and Yeovil Times* for 29 May 1855 and as it does not seem to have been noted previously, is quoted here in full:

> In consequence of the removal of the old school adjoining the church, it has been found necessary to repair the buttress at the south west angle of the tower. Mr. Short, the architect, under the direction of the churchwardens having examined it, recommended a complete restoration of the dilapidated buttress, in order to render it uniform with the others, and for the protection of the tower. This reparation is now taking place under Mr. Short's direction by Mr. Harwood mason of the town. We understand it will cost about £80. The ground on which the school stood appears not to have been at all used as a place of sepulture but the site of the old Engine House appears to have been so used, as workmen digging for a foundation have disturbed many relics of the dead. It is evident that the tower of the present church was erected subsequently to the school house and the removal of the latter to the present site was on many accounts desirable. The new school house we believe nearly approaches completion and will be both a credit and an ornament to the town.

This is important as it reveals that the proximity of the chantry to the tower buttress meant that the removal of the former necessitated the repair of the latter, and also for the comment that the tower had been built subsequent to the chantry and not the other way round. However, even more significant is the comment about the lack of evidence of burials, where the chantry had stood. The site of the chantry, therefore, must have been built over, or set aside from the rest of the churchyard, at a very early stage. Since the former is the more likely explanation, this means that the chantry either replaced an earlier building of the same ground plan (perhaps an early church) or was itself an adaptation of one. Vickery reported the discovery of a stone coffin 'underneath the west buttress of the building, and two or three feet beneath the surface.' This is the only example recorded in Yeovil and since stone coffins were only used in high-status burials, indicates that a single important burial had been disturbed by the building or modification of the chantry. Unfortunately, the coffin was not preserved.

The tower has prominent buttresses and on the north and west faces, these are of four stages, widening at each step to a broad base. On the south side, they are of only three stages, with the lowest increment omitted *(29)*. Consequently, they are proportionately narrower, an unusual anomaly requiring explanation. The position of the chantry abutting the westernmost of these narrow buttresses may provide the explanation since some antiquarian drawings show that the full width of the lowest stage would have blocked light to the east window of the chantry. This was likely to have been a window with an expensive scheme of painted glass, intended to provide one of the focal points of the chapel. The implication of this is that the buttresses on the south side of the tower were deliberately modified for the benefit of the chantry. A word of caution needs to be added here, since as well as the 1855 repairs, there was a major restoration of the tower in 1891, which included repair to the buttresses but this is unlikely to have resulted in any remodelling of their profiles.

Amongst the interesting discoveries made when the chantry was taken down, was a carved wooden shield acting as a roof boss (now lost). The local historian John Batten believed that it displayed the arms of Wynford, the family which owned the manor of Brympton D'Evercy from about 1365 until the mid-fifteenth century. Similar arms appear on a shield on the rood beam above the chancel screen, in Yeovil's daughter church at Brympton and Alice Wynford co-founded a chantry at Yeovil in the 1430s. It has been suggested that William Wynford, the likely architect of the present church, was a member of this family (even if not the Brympton branch). It is therefore tempting to speculate that he was directly involved in the decision to preserve the chapel, and adjusted his design accordingly.

Returning to the chantry in its original position, several contemporary illustrations provide useful information. The earliest, dating from about 1750, shows schoolboys marching in procession from their schoolroom, towards the church.

29 Tower of St John's, showing narrower buttresses on the south side, designed to accommodate the Chantry. © *B. and M. Gittos*

The south wall has two pointed and three rectangular windows, a doorway towards the west, a small chimney also at the west end and a series of stepped buttresses. The east end of the building is seen to be roughly in line with the adjacent tower buttress. The main windows are divided by a mullion and transom into four panes. These details are confirmed in an engraving published in the *Gentleman's Magazine* in 1824 which also shows the Engine House, constructed in 1812. Strangely this is not shown in Buckler's painting, apparently of 1817 which, despite appearing accurate, also omits all the rectangular windows in the south wall. However, it does include the large, blocked, east window partially obscured by the tower buttress. Buckler's painting also includes a string course around the chapel matching one of the string courses on the tower. This is not shown on the other drawings and may have been another of Buckler's 'improvements'. Wheatley's painting of 1847 has the blocked east window but is inaccurate in showing the chapel's east wall forward of the tower buttress and the Engine House not completely filling the gap. An engraving of around 1850 seems to be the most accurate depiction of the arrangement immediately prior to demolition, but what none of these illustrations portray is the far (north) side of the building and this is unfortunate, since it may have been less altered than the more visible side. Changes were evidently made at various times, reflecting developing use of the building. The small, rectangular windows and the chimney had, presumably, been added when it was converted to a school, together with the blocking of the east window. There appears to have been a small aperture in the blocking, towards its top, which could represent a further change. The plain fenestration of the two new windows on the south side would not have been original and at one time, an additional floor was inserted. The buttressing of the two southern corners, seen in these illustrations, appears similar to that of the new church, an arrangement characteristic of the work of William Wynford and, therefore, likely to have been a modification at the time St John's was built. All this creates considerable uncertainty about the original appearance of the chapel.

THE ANGLO-SAXON CHURCH PRECINCT

In searching for the lost Anglo-Saxon church it is useful to investigate the reasons for choosing the particular location. An important consideration would have been the availability of suitable water. The church's dedication to St John the Baptist emphasises the role of the minster church in the sacrament of baptism. Yeovil is fortunate in having water available not only from the River Yeo and its many tributary streams but also from springs and through sinking wells. Just to the north-east of the present church, in Silver Street, there was formerly a water source known as 'Nun's Well', which is believed to have been so-called because of the church's involvement, from the fifteenth century, with the Convent of Syon in Middlesex. However, this could have been the renaming of an existing holy well or spring which had always been in that location and would have added greatly to the attractiveness of this particular place for the establishment of a minster church.

Mick Aston has drawn attention to the tendency for a proportion of Anglo-Saxon settlements to be established upon some form of promontory. In the light of this, the choice of location for Yeovil's church is particularly interesting. On the east side there is a significant drop to the level of Silver Street, the lower part of which was formerly called Stairs Lane, reflecting the steepness of the approach from the east. There is another abrupt fall to the north along the former Sheep Lane (now North Lane). Although hidden by buildings, there is also a sharp ground fall to the south, which became visible when Lloyds Bank was rebuilt in 1989 (see Chapter 1). This enabled the full height of the southern boundary wall round the car park in front of Church House to be appreciated for the first time. This southern boundary can be traced through to Princes Street via nineteenth-century property boundaries. There is no obvious western topographical boundary but the alignment of Princes Street itself is sufficient to be able to draw an approximately square boundary for the precinct of the Saxon minster which would provide a symmetrical enclosure around the lost church, if it stood to the west of the present building *(30)*. This arrangement would locate the present church, in its cramped situation, on the very edge of the minster precinct. Theresa Hall's work on the minster churches of Dorset has found that the precincts in her study area are predominantly rectilinear in form. Elsewhere, curvilinear precincts are the norm, with rectilinear planning confined to minsters which reuse Roman structures. Yeovil's precinct is not only rectilinear but also aligned with the church and, therefore, appears to be part of the Dorset pattern. The difficulty of positioning the new church at Yeovil might be paralleled elsewhere and it would be worth investigating the case of Yetminster. Here, the fourteenth and fifteenth-century church is sited very close to the southern edge of its churchyard, with what appears to be ample free space in the centre of the plot. Perhaps another minster church was left standing whilst the replacement was being built.

Without archaeological investigation there is uncertainty about the arrangement and number of buildings within the precinct but there is a hint from a thirteenth-century document that the complexity might have been greater than so far envisaged. The Cartulary of Muchelney Abbey contains a charter which is undated but probably of the 1240s, concerning property in 'Puthlane' (now Middle Street) in the town of Yeovil 'which is of the tenement of the greater church of that town'. The use of the comparative 'greater' suggests more than one church and although this could be to distinguish it from the chapel of Kingston, it is more likely to have been used because there was more than one church within the minster precinct at Yeovil. This would certainly add to the crowded nature of the site and help to account for the awkward positioning of St John's. The occurrence of multiple churches in a pre-Conquest

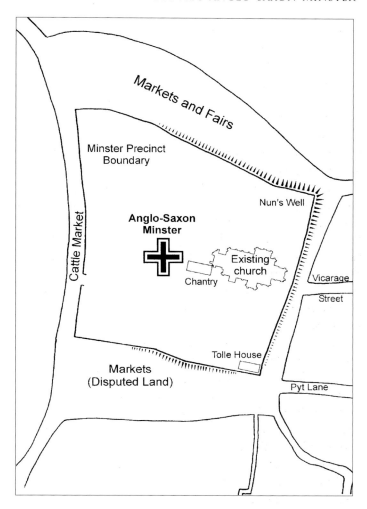

30 Plan of the Anglo-Saxon minster precinct, drawing together the available evidence.
© *B. and M. Gittos*

churchyard would not have been unusual, indeed at Christchurch (Hampshire) nine churches and many other buildings within the cemetery had to be demolished to make way for the grand Romanesque building which still stands.

The minster precinct can also be recognised by the evidence for the activities which became established around it. There is record of a dispute in 1364 between Robert de Samborne and 'certain townsmen' which resulted in a trial to establish whether the market stalls of 31 townsmen were on waste ground (the jurisdiction of which was claimed by Samborne) or on the king's highway. It seems likely that the disputed area lay between the present High Street and the southern precinct boundary, and the fact that Samborne won his case would explain why there are no properties of the Portreeve and Burgesses recorded on that side of the High Street (as Leslie Brooke has clearly shown in his map of the medieval borough). If the post-medieval buildings on the north side of the High Street are swept away, the High Street/Borough area becomes an impressively large market place along the southern boundary of the precinct. The land to the north of the precinct had long been used for fairs and markets and Princes Street, to the west, was traditionally the cattle market. Even the top of Silver Street has been used as a corn market. Gerard describes the market as 'one of the greatest I have seene' in a 'little towne' and he emphasises its long pedigree by stating that 'King John transferred the Sunday market to a Friday market'.

The Anglo-Saxon minster seems to have been established on a virgin, elevated site (no Roman finds have been reported from this area of the town) with markets and fairs on the open ground round the minster precinct, together with the 'tenement' providing the nucleus of the town. It must be significant that the only Anglo-Saxon pottery found so far in the town came from the site of Marks and Spencer, opposite the precinct (see Chapter 1). The creation of this trading centre, near to but not on the Roman road south from Ilchester, evidently caused a new route to be made through the town such that the old Roman road, relegated to a kind of bypass, ceased to be used, fell into decay and became totally lost at an early date *(31)*. This is responsible for the difficulty in tracing the course of the Roman road west of the town. Similar relationships between other Anglo-Saxon towns and lost Roman roads can be seen, for example, at Malmesbury and Hereford.

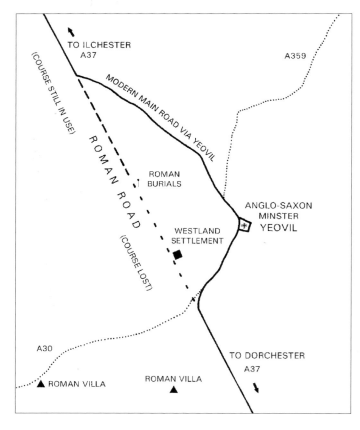

31 Relationship between the Anglo-Saxon minster and the Roman road from Ilchester to Dorchester. The principal Roman sites are also marked.
© *B. and M. Gittos*

THE MINSTER *PAROCHIA*

A useful starting point for reconstructing Yeovil's minster parish is the locations of its daughter churches. Their distribution needs to be seen in relation to the Anglo-Saxon administrative areas known as hundreds, which can often be shown to occupy areas similar to those of minster parishes. Many of Yeovil's daughter churches fall outside the bounds of Stone, where Yeovil itself is situated, extending into the neighbouring hundreds of Tintinhull, Coker and Houndsborough. There has been a tendency for larger hundreds to be divided into smaller units and, therefore, it is reasonable to propose that all four were originally a single unit and that this corresponded with the original minster parish. The map *(32)* shows the proposed minster parish for Yeovil assembled on this basis. Unfortunately, the precise boundaries of Anglo-Saxon hundreds are not recorded and the best which can be readily achieved is by using the modern boundaries of parishes which were located in each. However, it is

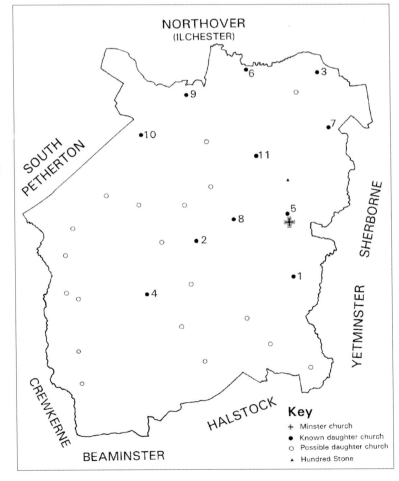

32 Map showing the probable extent of the minster parish of St John's. Daughter churches:
1 Barwick
2 Brympton D'Evercy
3 Chilton Cantelo
4 Chinnock
5 Kingston
6 Limington
7 Mudford
8 Preston
9 Sock Dennis
10 Tintinhull
11 Yeovil Marsh
© B. and M. Gittos

possible to check the general validity of the resulting minster parish by reviewing the territories which have been claimed for neighbouring *parochiae*. Katherine Barker has established the parish for the Anglo-Saxon cathedral church of Sherborne and this confirms the boundary to the east. Although not much is known about the minster at Yetminster, the place name is sufficiently suggestive and the present parish adjoins our minster parish to the south east. Marie Eedle has described the extent of the Beaminster *parochia*, which would have had only a short boundary with Yeovil, between North and South Perrott. The minster at Crewkerne, to the south-west, has been researched by Bob Dunning and on the far side of the Fosse Way, was the territory of South Petherton's minster. To the north, one of the churches at Ilchester (St Andrew's Northover) seems to have enjoyed minster status but its area of influence is rather uncertain. The proposed minster parish for Yeovil lies neatly between these neighbouring areas and, without it, there would be a significant gap left unexplained.

SURVIVING EVIDENCE

Having established that there was almost certainly an Anglo-Saxon church and that it was demolished some 600 years ago when the new church was built, can anything be recognised as surviving from it? One possible candidate was discovered in 1988, after the demolition of an unusual building in the grounds of Church House, immediately to the south of the churchyard. This was a small, anonymous structure attached to the buildings on the east side of the forecourt. It had a cellar and a highly irregular ground plan but its importance lay in the fact that the stone walls contained much reused material. This was sorted through by members of the Yeovil Archaeological and Local History Society and, amongst the worked stones, were found the heads and sills of two unglazed fourteenth-century windows and a fragmentary head from a very simple, round-headed window *(33)*. It showed considerable weathering and it is possible that this may have come from an Anglo-Saxon building. In the previous year, a more remarkable discovery had been made, when the new Belmont Street southern relief road was being put through (see Chapter 1). Careful cleaning of this cylindrical object showed it to be a piece of Ham stone with grooves around it, narrower and broken at one end *(colour plate 3)*. The opposite end has a square, central, recess. The stone has been turned on a lathe and the recess at the thicker end is one of the support points. The object would originally have been about twice as long as it is now, with the broken end at roughly the middle. This would give an overall length of approximately 29in (0.74m) and a diameter of 6in (152mm). In trying to understand this object, many possible uses were considered. Was it an industrial roller or an architectural detail from a Roman building? Turned Ham stone capitals and bases are known from the Roman villa at Halstock just to the south of Yeovil but their

33 Broken, unglazed, round-headed window head discovered amongst the Church House stones.
© *B. and M. Gittos*

character is fundamentally different. This piece appears to have been simply a short shaft decorated with a pattern of grooves and narrower at its centre. It is difficult to find close parallels for the Yeovil stone but comparisons can made with pre-Conquest fragments from the Old Minster at Winchester and Canterbury Cathedral. This points to an Anglo-Saxon origin for the piece. Comments were sought from relevant experts and Professor Rosemary Cramp confirmed this as the most likely explanation. Baluster shafts were used in Anglo-Saxon church towers to divide the openings in the belfry (particularly in the north of England). However, they could have other functions such as in arcading as at St Alban's Abbey or as part of church furnishings. The small scale of the Yeovil shaft perhaps makes the latter more likely. Whatever its original use, it must have come from a major Anglo-Saxon building and provides tangible evidence for the existence of the minster at Yeovil.

The importance of the baluster as a piece of Anglo-Saxon carving can be appreciated in relation to Sally Foster's survey of Anglo-Saxon sculpture in historic Somerset. She focused on the decorated carving, but did give a brief summary of surviving architectural stone-work and commented 'The scarcity highlights how paltry are the actual remains of either standing or destroyed Anglo-Saxon architecture in Somerset'. There is even less material in Devon and Cornwall and relatively little in Dorset. There are no recorded examples of Anglo-Saxon balusters from any of the south-western counties and the nearest *in situ* examples are probably at North Leigh, Oxfordshire. Half-round and grooved shafts can be seen high up in the crossing, beneath the tower at Sherborne Abbey but this appears to be Romanesque decoration. It is at Sherborne that the only other known example of the use of Ham stone in the pre-Conquest period is to be found, where it has been used to create the hood moulding around the surviving early doorway in the west front. In the immediate vicinity of Yeovil, there are cross shaft fragments at West Camel and Yetminster but these are carved from oolitic limestone, probably from the Bath area. This material was favoured by Anglo-Saxon stone carvers and its use for the Hundred Stone (in Mudford Road, Yeovil) strongly suggests a pre-Conquest origin for it (see *23*). The broken and weathered recess in the top of the surviving section of the Hundred Stone points to its having been part of a larger structure, with blocks held together by dowels. This method of assembly was common for pre-Conquest crosses. Undecorated Anglo-Saxon stonework occurs in the quoins at the west end of St Michael's church East Coker, but again, oolitic limestone seems to have been utilised for the most part. By any criterion, therefore, the Yeovil baluster is an important addition to the limited evidence not only for the church of Yeovil but also for Anglo-Saxon masonry in the south-west of England.

CONCLUSION

The case for an early church at Yeovil is now established. It seems to have been functioning as a minster by the mid-tenth century, having been founded on a favourable, elevated, site where abundant water was available from nearby springs. Several daughter churches can be identified, which demonstrate the minster's sphere of influence and allow a boundary to be drawn between the Yeovil minster parish and that of the adjoining minsters at South Petherton, Crewkerne, Yetminster, Ilchester (Northover) and the cathedral church at Sherborne. Yeovil's minster may have had a bell tower and at some stage in its history, a separate chapel was built in its churchyard. The minster probably stood immediately west of the present church, which explains the latter's awkward topographical situation. It is likely to have survived until the late fourteenth century, when it was replaced by a major new building in the emerging Perpendicular style. The minster church was established on a greenfield site and the nucleus of a small, associated market town was already detectable by the time of the Domesday survey. The controversial dual role of the rector, as lord of the town and incumbent of the church was due to a specific grant of privileges but also reflected the importance of the church as the main focus of the town. The form of the fourteenth-century town seal carrying the dedication of the church rather than the name of the town, demonstrates the lasting effect of such authority.

CHAPTER 4

CASTLE, CHURCH AND CONQUEST:
THE NORMANS IN SOUTH SOMERSET

Sally Mills

THE CONQUEST AND THE CASTLE

On 14 October 1066 William the Bastard, Duke of Normandy, defeated Harold Godwinson, King of England, at Hastings. Henceforth William would be named 'the Conqueror' and two months later, on Christmas Day, he was crowned at Westminster. William's kingdom had been won by the sword and the swords had been wielded by his supporters. Now, they too, sought their reward. William divided England between a handful of men such as Bishop Odo of Bayeux, Robert of Mortain and Alan the Red, from Brittany. These men and their lines would subsequently become great magnates. Lands in 20 counties, including a vast swathe of south-western England, were granted to Robert, Count of Mortain (near Avranches). This included land in Yeovil and the estate at Montacute. Robert, like Bishop Odo of Bayeux was William the Conqueror's half-brother. The Norman Conquest was kept very much within the family.

The Count of Mortain's first priority was securing his rule in the lands that his half-brother had granted him. He did this in much the same way as William secured the country, by building castles to act as strongholds and power bases and by sharing his lands with his own loyal followers. The Count built one of his castles on a hill by the settlement known before the Conquest as Bishopston. At this time, the castle site was named *Montagud* (which simply means 'steep hill') and the village is still known by this name, Montacute, today. The site of the castle is now masked by heavy tree cover *(34)* but the mound of the motte and the ditch surrounding the bailey are still discernible on the ground to the careful eye. It was from here that Robert, Count of Mortain, ruled his fiefdom.

34 The 'steep hill' of Montacute where a miraculous image of Christ was supposedly discovered, *c.*1030. The earthworks of William the Conqueror's half brother's castle crown its summit. From *Gentleman's Magazine*, 1817

Montacute does not appear, at first sight, to have been the most obvious choice for Robert's castle. He could have built his motte and bailey within the northern spur of Ham Hill, secured by great Iron Age defences already over 1000 years old. Many of his peers did exactly this, as at Old Sarum, near Salisbury in Wiltshire. Yet he chose not to and placed his castle on the smaller summit of a separate hill to the east. One explanation for this choice may lie in Kissmedown Lane, today part of the Leland Way but arguably Roman in origin. This route links Montacute with Ilchester and, through the Fosse Way, with the country's network of main roads (based on the Roman system). But Ham Hill itself overlooks the Fosse Way, so the choice cannot simply have been dictated by the presence of a convenient communications route. It seems likely that the hill had a very special significance in the eleventh century.

The *Waltham Chronicle*, written around 1177, describes a miraculous discovery on the summit of Montacute. It records that in the reign of Cnut (1016-35), a great lord named Tovi unearthed a magical life-size image of Christ on the hill, following a visionary dream by a local blacksmith. Tovi promised this and other holy relics to the great churches of London, Winchester, Canterbury, Glastonbury and Reading. However, when Tovi tried to remove the icon from Montacute, the 24 oxen yoked to the cart on which the statue was loaded, refused to move. Eventually, Tovi suggested taking the statue to his estate and church at Waltham, in Essex (now Waltham Abbey). As soon as he said the name 'Waltham', the cart began to move and after its long journey, the statue was safely installed in Tovi's church at Waltham.

After Tovi's death, his lands eventually passed to Harold Godwinson and the *Waltham Chronicle* records how, before the Battle of Hastings, he prayed in front of the statue. However, as Harold left the church, the image of Christ is said to have 'bowed its head as if in sorrow' – an ill omen. After Harold's defeat at Hastings, the clergymen at Waltham claimed to have recovered his body and buried it in their church.

In many respects we may well be sceptical about this story, with its visionary dream, miraculous statue and oxen refusing to move until it was decided to take the cross to Waltham. However, this kind of story was both acceptable and expected in the Middle Ages, when miracles were part of the culture. Indeed, Tovi is quite likely to have engineered the entire affair, in order to endow his church with a precious relic. This would have given him personal prestige and ensured that his church received plenty of donations from other rich patrons and pilgrims, wishing to secure their place in heaven. Despite the dubious credibility of the story itself, the discovery of the Montacute statue is likely to have been a real, if engineered, event and Tovi was certainly a historical figure, for he is mentioned in other documents dating from the reign of Cnut. Furthermore, relic manufacture was big business in the Middle Ages, and frequently practised, most famously, perhaps, by the monks of Glastonbury Abbey, when they claimed to have discovered the graves of the legendary King Arthur and his Queen, Guinevere, in 1191.

The story of the miraculous discovery at Montacute is relevant for two reasons. In the first place, it gives the hill a very special significance, already established at the time of the Norman Conquest. Secondly, Waltham Abbey and the image of Christ were associated with Harold Godwinson, the last Anglo-Saxon king. This connection with Harold would have provided Robert, Count of Mortain, with a good reason for choosing to build his castle on Montacute. It was an affront to Harold's memory, and an action that can have left no doubt as to who was now in control.

What do we know of Robert, Count of Mortain? One ancient source describes Robert as '*crassi et hebetis ingenii*' or stupid and dull, while another recounts that he was a wife beater. While he may have been a violent man, the idea that a stupid, dull man would be entrusted with vast estates and important military operations by the Conqueror does not entirely ring true. Before the Conquest, Montacute had belonged to Athelney Abbey. Robert acquired this estate in exchange for land at Purse Caundle in Dorset. Montacute was a valuable estate, worth over £9 per annum. Purse Caundle, however, was worth less than £4. Robert made the better deal, hardly the action of a dullard, while the Abbey lost out. Furthermore, during the great rebellion in 1068, Robert was fighting alongside his half-brother in the north, while his castle at Montacute was besieged unsuccessfully by the men of Somerset. It seems that comments about Robert's dull nature are the product of attempts to discredit him, once he and his son had fallen from grace.

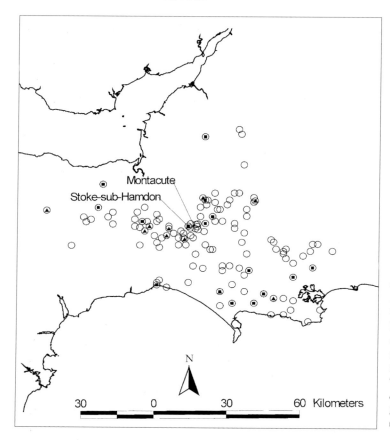

35 The distribution of the Count of Mortain's estates in Somerset and Dorset. Squares are estates granted by the Count to Robert fitz Ivo. Triangles indicate estates held by Mauger de Cartrai. © Sally Mills

More is known of Robert's followers. The great survey of 1086, known to us as the Domesday Book, recorded all land holdings in the country for tax purposes. From this source, can be discovered the names and often the positions of the most important men in the Count's household. The map (35) shows the Count's holdings in Somerset and Dorset, as revealed by the Domesday Book, including the estates granted by him to his henchmen. Chief among these was Alfred, or Alured, who was the Count's butler. It is likely that Alured was responsible for the administration of all the Count's estates in England. He was well rewarded for this work for, although many of the Count's household were rich and powerful men in their own right, Alured seems to have been the richest and most powerful. Another of importance was Robert fitz Ivo, also known as Robert the Constable. His role was to maintain law and order and to ensure the security of the Count's residences. Ansgar the Breton, also known as Ansgar the Cook, is unlikely to have been just a cook. It is more probable that he was responsible for provisioning and running the Count's kitchens and storerooms. Finally there were the *milites*, or knights, like Bretel, Drogo and Mauger de Cartrai. All of these men, the Count's loyal followers, held land in Montacute or in the surrounding villages.

Robert fitz Ivo, the constable of Montacute, held his largest and most valuable estates at Stoke sub Hamdon. He had two land holdings here, valued at £7 and £2. In the late eleventh century, this was a significant sum and it is almost identical to the value of Mortain's own castle and lands at Montacute, which were worth £9 3s in 1086. Thus, at Stoke sub Hamdon, one of the Count's chief vassals was established with great favour. Fitz Ivo's line was to become one of the most important and influential families in the area throughout the medieval period. His son, Robert de Bello Campo, gave his name to all his descendants, who were thereafter known as Beauchamp. Both Shepton and Hatch Beauchamp derive their names from the Beauchamps. Until the late fourteenth century, the Beauchamp family had a major residence at what is now the main village centre, formerly known as West Stoke. This comprised a fortified manor house and a collegiate chapel.

THE CHURCH

Isolated today, to the east of Stoke sub Hamdon, is the smaller settlement of East Stoke. It is dominated by the parish church of St Mary the Virgin, which stands on the south side of the village (colour plate 6). The church, like so many English parish churches, is the product of a millennium of changes and restorations but, despite this, it retains much of its early character. It is, in essence, still very much a Norman building of simple nave and chancel. In this largely secular age, conditioned by more than 400 years of Protestantism, it is difficult to imagine the medieval church in its full glory, when it would have been decorated throughout with paintings and sculpture, every surface richly coloured. The decoration of Norman churches, in particular, would have been quite alien to modern eyes.

It is fortunate that the church at Stoke sub Hamdon is adorned with particularly fine Norman sculpture, something which could only have been afforded by a wealthy patron. It is for this carving that the church is best known. In particular, it has an elaborate corbel table, intriguing tympanum above the north door and a noteworthy chancel arch. A corbel table is formed by a series of projecting stones (corbels) which are part of the building structure intended to support the roof. In the Norman period, these blocks of stone are typically carved with wide-ranging and complex designs, which include geometric motifs although human figures, animals and fantastic monsters also abound. The corbel table of the church of St Mary the Virgin survives only on the north and south sides of the chancel. Originally, it would also have adorned the nave, but later rebuilding of this part of the church has all but destroyed it. A single stone from the nave corbel table survives, now inside the church, above the arch to the south chapel. Most of the surviving chancel corbels are carved with geometric designs. However, one on the south side shows a running hare, perhaps a reference to hunting, a favourite pastime of the Norman elite *(colour plate 7)*. Two other corbels, one on each side of the chancel, show wheat ears, an obvious symbol of plenty but perhaps the most striking and alien of the surviving corbels is a so-called Sheila-na-Gig, which has been described as one of the finest in the country *(36)*. A Sheila-na-Gig is a grotesque carving of a naked female figure posing in a manner which displays and emphasises the genitalia. Although this is not the sort of imagery that we would now associate with the Church, it was acceptable in medieval culture. In an illiterate age, it may have been intended to serve as a warning against lust, the fifth of the seven deadly sins or, alternatively, as a symbol of fertility.

Over the north door is an elaborately carved, semi-circular stone known as a tympanum *(37)*, a panel used to fill the space between the arched head and the flat lintel of a Norman doorway. There are many examples of carved tympana in England, but only six others in Somerset. That at Stoke sub Hamdon has often been noted for its unusual design. Its central feature is the Tree of Life and this has three birds, of differing sizes, perching on it. On the upper right, facing towards the Tree of Life, is an *Agnus Dei*, or Lamb of God. Below this is a creature labelled 'LEO', facing in the opposite direction. Presumably he is supposed to be a lion, although it has been noted that he looks more like an ass, his ears being unusually long. Lions usually represent strength and courage but this one appears to be slinking away from a centaur (on the opposite side), preparing to shoot him with an arrow. The centaur, labelled 'SAGITARIVS', is used occasionally in Norman art. Although the exact significance of this particular composition is lost to us, it would undoubtedly have been understood by its Norman spectators.

The Norman chancel arch *(38)* which, like the tympanum and the corbel table, probably dates from between about 1100 and 1130, is of three orders, decorated with simple geometric designs. They comprise a pattern made up of diagonal crosses, chevron (a simple zigzag motif) and billet moulding (a double

36 Left The Sheila-na-Gig on the corbel table at Stoke sub Hamdon. Does it promote fertility or warn of the dangers of lust? © *B. and M. Gittos*

37 Opposite above The tympanum over the north door at Stoke sub Hamdon showing the Lamb of God and Tree of Life (centre) with Sagittarius (left) and Leo (right). © *B. and M. Gittos*

38 Opposite below The Norman chancel arch at Stoke sub Hamdon. *Drawing by J. Buckler, courtesy Somerset Archaeological and Natural History Society*

band of short, alternating half-cylinders). Billet now decorates the outer edge of the chancel arch and was added by the diocesan architect, Benjamin Ferrey, during the course of his restoration of the church in 1862. This was to replace carving which had been 'hacked off' and for the same reason Ferrey also provided new capitals, from which the arch now springs. Buckler's illustration, of 1835, shows the arch before restoration but although now much altered, it still retains of its original character.

So what would the church have looked like in the Norman period? Imagine approaching the building from the north. The church dominates your view, framed against the wooded slopes of Ham Hill, which rises behind it. The church is not the golden colour of Ham stone, as it is today, but gleams whitely with limewash in the morning sun. The brightly painted figures on the corbel table look down on the approaching visitor. Having absorbed this view, you enter the building through the porchless north door. Over the door the tympanum is gorgeously painted and the letters of its inscription picked out, probably in red. It is protected from the elements by a stone canopy (like the more elaborate example at Lullington, near Frome) which rises above it. Set within the canopy is a niche cut into the wall which holds an image of the church's patron saint (this niche is still visible from the first floor room of the porch today).

Having entered the church, heavy with the smell of incense, you find yourself directly opposite the south door (now blocked). To your modern eyes the church looks empty, since there are no pews. At this time the congregation all stood. However, the walls are covered with paintings of figures and geometric designs. Few traces of these paintings survive at Stoke today but clear fragments of a Norman decorative scheme survive at nearby Sutton Bingham. Turning left, your view is dominated by the beautiful chancel arch which is also brightly painted. The chancel arch divides the secular space of the nave from the sacred and holy space of the chancel, where the altar stands and the priest says mass. Beyond this arch, the chancel can be seen to end in a semi-circular apse, not square as it is today. Between you and the chancel arch stands the Norman font, now to be seen opposite the north door. This font is still in use today and similar examples exist at Sutton Bingham and East Coker. It may not be going too far to suggest that these fonts could be the products of the same mason. The whole building is lit by a series of narrow, slit, windows (three of which still survive). There is no tower or south transept and no large windows. It is a simpler building but one no less imposing than the modified structure you see today.

THE MANOR OF ROBERT FITZ IVO?

It is clear that the Norman church at Stoke sub Hamdon was a building designed to impress. Who could have built such an expensive structure? As is clear from the Domesday Book, two of the Count of Mortain's chief men held

39 A small window in the south wall of the nave. This window is very similar to an example from Great Hale, Lincolnshire, dated to 1050-1100.
© *Sally Mills*

estates at Stoke sub Hamdon, Mauger de Cartrai and Robert fitz Ivo. Is it possible that one of these men built the church? Initially, this seems unlikely, as the fine Norman features discussed above belong to the early twelfth century. If Mauger and Robert both came over to England in the Conquest of 1066, by 1100, even if they were still alive, they would have been old men, particularly by the standards of the day. However, all is not as it appears at the church, for there is evidence that the original church dates from before this time.

This evidence is demonstrated by the small windows that still survive in the walls of the church *(39)*. Whereas the corbel table, tympanum and chancel arch are all good examples of twelfth-century work, these windows are more characteristic of eleventh-century craftsmanship. They have a close parallel at the church of St John the Baptist at Great Hale in Lincolnshire, which has been dated to the period 1050-1100. There is also a curious carving, known as the Dragon Slayer *(40 and 41)*, over a narrow window on the north side of the nave. The date of this piece is a subject of some controversy. Stylistically, it does not compare favourably with Norman depictions of St Michael or St George, both popular themes of the twelfth century. However, given its subject matter, it is not likely to be earlier than the eleventh century, as carvings of this type are virtually unknown before then. Two commentators on the church, Pevsner and Ashdown, have also noted that this piece would fit more comfortably before the year 1100 than after it.

Almost certainly, therefore, the church at Stoke sub Hamdon was originally built before the twelfth century. The 'Norman' work can then be seen as an

40 Left The mysterious dragon slayer carving as drawn by William Walter in 1849. *Courtesy Somerset Archaeological and Natural History Society*

41 Above The dragon slayer today. Its date is hotly disputed but it is likely to have been carved before 1100. © *B. and M. Gittos*

embellishment, rather than a major building programme. However, this is not to say that the church is of Saxon origin. Instead, it was probably built in the difficult overlap period between Saxon and Norman styles, in the second half of the eleventh century. It is likely, therefore, that the original church *was* built by Mauger de Cartrai or Robert fitz Ivo, not long after the Conquest and soon after the construction of Mortain's castle at Montacute. Mauger can probably be discounted as the builder of the church. His main estates were not at Stoke sub Hamdon and his lands here seem only to have served to provide him with a base close to Montacute. For Robert fitz Ivo, however, the situation was very different. He had two estates at Stoke, one of which was his principal (and most valuable) land holding. If he were to have built an expensive church anywhere, it would have been here.

There is further evidence in support of this hypothesis. By the late eleventh century, a system of parish churches was already in being throughout England and new churches were then being built beside manor houses, enhancing the status of the local lord. This is the case, for example, at Sutton Bingham, where the manor house stands to this day, just south of the church. Unlike Sutton Bingham, there are now no buildings to be seen south of the church at Stoke. Indeed, several archaeologists have noted the odd isolation of the church in relation to the modern village. However, this mystery is solved by consulting a map made in 1776 and an aerial photograph taken in 1966.

The map made of Stoke sub Hamdon parish, by William Simpson in 1776, shows a landscape of which only the bones survive today *(42a)*. The medieval

42a The roads and fields around the church at Stoke sub Hamdon, c.1776. Redrawn from Dunning, 1974

42b The roads and fields around Stoke sub Hamdon as they may have looked c.1100. Note the change in alignment of the southern road to serve the possible manor site. Redrawn from Dunning, 1974

pattern of strip fields is depicted just prior to the enclosure acts of the late eighteenth and early nineteenth centuries. The main road from east to west, running from Yeovil to South Petherton, is still in use today. In 1776, as it approached the outskirts of Stoke sub Hamdon, it split into two branches which rejoined, just below the point on Ham Hill where the war memorial stands today. This is a very odd road layout and some explanation for it must

43 An aerial photograph of the church and possible manor site (A). Note the linear marks, probably a road, running south along the west edge of the churchyard and into the enclosures beyond (arrowed). Is this the manor of Robert fitz Ivo? © *Crown copyright 1966. All rights reserved. WL7117*

be sought. Just before the roads rejoin on the 1776 map, the southern route crosses a small field, divided into the characteristic strips of medieval agriculture. Interestingly, the road cuts across these strips at an angle, suggesting that this section of the route has been added later. So it is plausible to suggest that the southern route did not always rejoin the other road. If this were the case, then what was its destination?

An aerial photograph, taken for the Ordnance Survey in 1966, may provide the answer (43). It shows a former road running in a north–south direction beyond the western boundary of the churchyard. This road seems to connect with an enclosure, partially preserved in the modern field boundaries. Within this enclosure there are hints on the aerial photograph of ancient occupation. Could this be the long vanished manor site of Robert fitz Ivo? If it were, then the southern branch of the main road through the village would originally have swung past the church and up to the manor (42b). Later, when the manor was abandoned, the road, which now led to a dead end, became diverted and carried on across the fields to rejoin the route to the west.

The final proof that this was fitz Ivo's manor site awaits confirmation. However, what is clear is that Stoke sub Hamdon and Montacute were once caught up with the new, Norman, ruling elite. The traces of their important medieval past can still be seen in the church at Stoke, on maps, aerial photographs and on the summit of St Michael's Hill (34). They remain as witnesses of the turbulent times after the Norman Conquest and the important role of southern Somerset in the eleventh century.

CHAPTER 5

THE ARCHAEOLOGY
OF THE LIBRARY SITE

Brian and Moira Gittos

INTRODUCTION

The examination of two town-centre plots in the 1980s transformed perceptions of Yeovil's archaeological potential and warrant special consideration. The survey in Chapter 1 shows that archaeological recording conducted by the YALHS on the site of Yeovil's new library was a pivotal event, a message which was reinforced by the findings from Petters House. In 1986 a replacement for Yeovil's old library in King George Street was long overdue and after some sixty years the County Council had agreed that Yeovil was to have a purpose-built library for the second time. Because of the central location of the chosen site, the YALHS decided it was necessary to mount an intensive watching brief. This began in the summer of 1986 by observing the initial site preparations and monitoring during the digging of foundation trenches *(44)*. Work was completed the following year when there was a second opportunity, this time to examine the area around the new building which had been protected by tarmac during the construction work. In parallel with this second season at the library, another watching brief was mounted a few hundred metres to the south, where preparations had begun for construction of Petters House.

Looking back, it is clear that the archaeological recording undertaken by the YALHS was the result of a happy coalescence of fortunate circumstances. The time was favourable because the currently inhibiting effects of public liability insurance and the Health and Safety at Work legislation had not yet taken effect. Similarly, the exclusion of amateur archaeology as a consequence of PPG 16 had not yet occurred. The Society members involved were able to devote the necessary time and the contractors were both sympathetic and proactively helpful. Curiously, at the time, there was little consensus as to the worth of carrying out archaeology in that area of the town. There was a

44 General view of the Library Site in 1986, looking south towards Petters Way. © *B. and M. Gittos*

45 Difficult conditions for archaeology. Brian Gittos traces the angled roadway on the Library Site while work is continuing all around. © *B. and M. Gittos*

popular belief that 'deep Victorian cellars' would have destroyed all the earlier deposits and that nothing of interest was left to be found. In the event, this pessimism proved to be unfounded and the evidence for Yeovil's past soon emerged. The recovery of so much information was all the more remarkable because no trenching or trial pitting was carried out *(45)*. It was the contractor's trenches which revealed the features and most of the finds. The new Public Library was to be built adjoining the old building, on a car park on the corner of South Street and King George Street, just within the limits of the medieval borough.

HISTORY OF THE LIBRARY SITE

The first maps which show useful information about the town date from the early nineteenth century, beginning with Mr Watts' map of 1806 but they do not contain accurate detail until after about 1850. Manuscript sources for the history of the area were researched by Leonard Hayward and Leslie Brooke, revealing that there was a public house called the King's Head at the northern extremity of the site, fronting the High Street. It is mentioned in the mid–eighteenth century as being formerly known as the 'Cock in the Hoop'. This was one of a group of four public houses which used to be situated along the south side of the High Street. There were also some cottages at the southern end of the site in South Street (known for a long period as Back Street). The King's Head was sold in 1848 together with some cottages and demolished to make way for Yeovil's new Town Hall and market complex, completed the following year. In 1857, plans were produced for building a new Corn Exchange and markets. They were to be erected on the site of the 'out premises' of the Bell Inn, South Street. These new buildings are shown on the first really detailed map available, dated 1858, which accompanied a report on the town's drainage. This map also shows the markets which then occupied most of the area, including a substantial Market fronting South Street. Some other important features are also shown on the 1858 map. They include the Hall Keeper's House (No.4 South Street) beside the Cheese Market but set back from the road; the course of a lane, known as George Court and another narrow roadway, running through the markets, parallel to George Court but a little to the west. The whole area is clearly shown on the best available nineteenth-century map: the 1:500 scale 1886 Ordnance Survey *(46)*. This also identifies a Meat Market between the Town Hall and the Cheese Market. Leslie Brooke's sketch of South Street *(47)*, based on a late nineteenth-century photograph shows the front of the Cheese Market, with its three arches and a narrow, three-storey shop adjoining it on the east side.

The next most important development was in 1915, when the Cheese Market was converted into the town's Fire Station *(48)*, which had previously

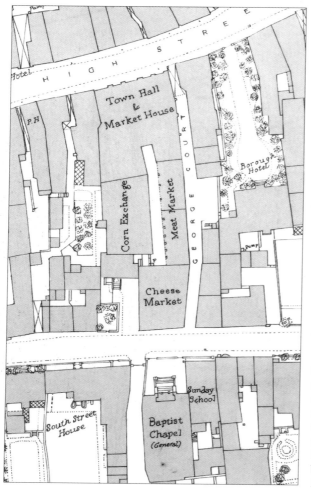

46 *Left* The area of the Library Site in 1886 showing the Cheese Market, Corn Exchange and Meat Market. *Redrawn by Leslie Brooke from the 1886 Ordnance Survey map*

47 *Opposite, above* Drawing looking west along South Street. The three arches in the middle distance belonged to the cheese market and there is a three-storey building alongside. Leslie Brooke after a late nineteenth-century photograph. © *Marjorie Brooke*

48 *Opposite, below* The Library Site prior to 1962, when the fire station was demolished. It retained one of the three arches of the cheese market visible in (47), and the entrance to the former markets towards the rear. The Hall Keeper's House is on the left in this sketch by Leslie Brooke. © *Marjorie Brooke*

occupied cramped premises in Vicarage Street. Major upheavals were to follow, with the construction of King George Street in the 1920s. This was a new road, linking South Street to the High Street, just east of George Court. With this new highway came the municipal offices, museum and former library which were built over George Court. The work was completed in 1928 only seven years before the Town Hall was burnt down. The Corn Exchange, situated immediately behind the Town Hall, was badly damaged by enemy bombing in the Second World War. A photograph, taken in April 1962, shows the Corn Exchange still standing but as a roofless, empty shell. Two other photographs, from the Cave Collection held by the Museum of South Somerset, show the Fire Station being demolished in 1962 and it is believed that the remains of the Corn Exchange also went at the same time. The cleared site was converted into a car park, with the children's library annexe and offices occupying the middle ground. Shops had earlier been built in the Borough, in place of the Town Hall

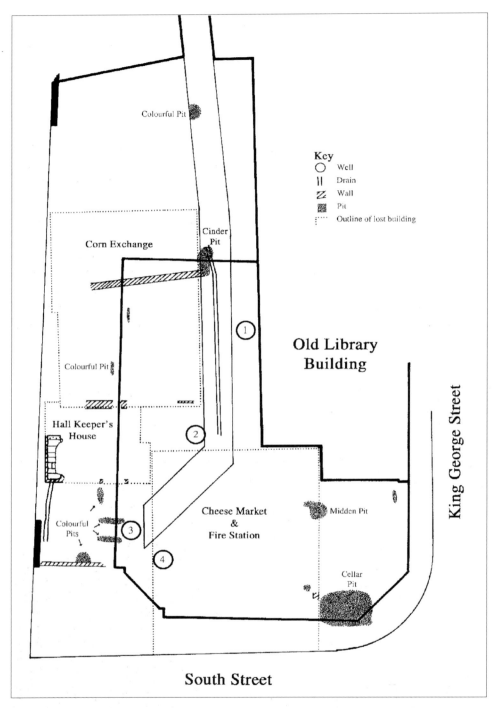

Key
○ Well
‖ Drain
Ƶ Wall
▧ Pit
⋯⋯ Outline of lost building

Colourful Pit

Corn Exchange

Cinder Pit

Old Library Building

King George Street

Colourful Pit

Hall Keeper's House

Cheese Market & Fire Station

Midden Pit

Colourful Pits

Cellar Pit

South Street

49 Plan of the Library Site showing the main features from both 1986 and 1987. The new building is the L-shaped outline in the centre. © *B. and M. Gittos*

and later, a public toilet was built, towards the High Street end of the plot. The archaeological evidence was found to fit well with the known history but it was also able to add more detail and pose some further questions.

THE FEATURES REVEALED

Work commenced on preparing the site in the late spring of 1986. The first feature was seen only by the contractors, who had fortunately photographed it because immediately below the tarmac was a complete cobbled lane, lying north–south, close to the west wall of the old library. This was the unnamed route through the markets, to the west of George Court. For this and other features noted during the investigation, see the plan *(49)*. At a later stage, more of the car park tarmac was stripped, to reveal another section of the course of the cobbled roadway which held something of a surprise. Instead of proceeding directly to meet South Street at right angles, it turned south-west and came to a well-defined end without ever reaching the road *(50)*. This metalled end of the roadway was the only complete part which could be examined in the first

50 Left View across the Library Site in 1986, looking along the course of the angled roadway towards South Street, with No.80 (the Community Arts Centre) in the background.
© *B. and M. Gittos*

51 Below Section through the drain below the cobbled roadway through the markets, with the Baptist church in South Street just visible behind. © *B. and M. Gittos*

season, the rest being rapidly removed by the contractor. The setts, however, were not discarded but were reused in the restoration of Church Path, Queen Camel. At its end, the road was flanked by short sections of shallow gutter although elsewhere it was edged with lines of bricks. The gutter was interrupted at one point by a square block of Ham stone, flush with the kerb.

Just east of the roadway and hard against the library wall, the first of four wells was discovered. Its rapid removal and consolidation by the contractors meant that little evidence could be gleaned from it, other than the fact that at least the top of the well was brick-lined. The alignment of the roadway was confirmed by the presence of a U-shaped drain (51), running below the centre of the road, at a depth of just over a foot (25cm). The 'U' section was wider towards the top. It was cut in several places by the contractor's trenches and at each point the same construction was evident. The sides and base were lined with brick and it was capped with slabs of Ham stone. The trench in which the drain had been laid had been limed and the drain itself contained silt which varied in content and depth along its length. Towards South Street, the drain had very little silt, whereas towards the High Street, it was more than half filled with a dark deposit. The contents of the silt varied along the drain's length and appeared to reflect different activities in the markets above. In one location there were many bone fragments, some of which had been sawn, suggesting waste from the Meat Market and in another position the fill was very sandy with fine scales, suggestive of fish. The most interesting artefact recovered from the drain was a tiny turned wooden disc with a central hole, possibly from a necklace.

A second well was discovered early in the trench-cutting sequence. It was situated on the west side of the cobbled roadway, opposite the corner of the old library and was entirely constructed from handmade bricks of a tapered design specially suited to well construction. Its well-head was broken up by the excavator but this was also of brick and probably rectangular. However, these bricks were of more modern appearance and it seemed that a new head had been added to an earlier well. Again the well was rapidly excavated and backfilled with concrete, giving no opportunity to assess its contents. About 50 of the handmade bricks were rescued from near the top of the well. Close to the southern end of the roadway, was the third well. Fortunately there was time to examine the top of this well which, unlike the previous two, was of Ham stone (52). However, there were only two or three courses of stone remaining around the well top and neither stone nor brick beneath. When this well was dug out by a mechanical excavator, it could be seen that it had been lined with clay, some of which fell away as it was excavated. It was removed to a depth of about 15ft (4.6m) but again there was no opportunity to examine the fill. On the penultimate day of the watching brief, just before the steel erectors moved in to begin the next phase of the construction, a fourth well was discovered, very close to the third and just west of the end of the cobbled roadway. Its top was not observed but it also appeared to be clay-lined.

52 Above, left The Ham stone top of well 3, after cleaning, near the end of the 1986 season on the Library Site. The Newnham Memorial Hall in South Street can also be seen. © *B. and M. Gittos*

53 Above, right Cleaning in progress on the long wall, at the north end of the Library Site. The cinder pit lay at the far end. © *B. and M. Gittos*

Trenches at the south-east corner showed, close to the surface, much burnt material of recent origin, which probably represented no more than bonfire residues from the Fire Station demolition. Nearby there was considerable disturbance, to a depth of about 15ft (4.6m). This was probably a filled-in cellar beneath the three-storey building noted above. Also in this area, the substantial footings of a stone wall, faced on its eastern side, were revealed. This was in the right position for it to be the east wall of the Cheese Market/Fire Station.

There is a step in the south wall of the old library building because it was constructed around the Fire Station and it remains as a mirror image of that part of the vanished building. It has also been perpetuated in the north wall of the new library. Just south of this step, the contractor's trenches revealed a fortunate discovery, a rubbish pit, datable by its contents to the early eighteenth century. It was christened the 'midden pit' and it produced almost as many artefacts (mostly pottery and glass) as the whole of the rest of the site put together! These included the two most complete vessels found, a small green-glazed ointment pot and 26 pieces of a chamber pot *(colour plate 11)*. The most substantial structure revealed by the excavations was a stone wall at the north end of the site. Its dimensions were at least 29ft 6in (8.8m) long by 4ft (1.2m) high *(53)*. The alignment was at right angles to the old library and more indicative of a building fronting the High Street than South Street. Near the base of this well-built wall was discovered an early example of one of the many clay pipes found distributed over the site. It belonged to the first half of the seventeenth century and provided dating evidence for the wall. The alignment and position of the wall did not correspond to any of the known buildings. It stopped at the edge of the roadway but was visible westwards to the limit of the excavations. Traces of two further east–west walls were noted. One corresponded to the southern end wall of the Corn Exchange and the other was probably the rear wall of the Hall Keeper's House. A matt, red, tiled floor was apparent just below the tarmac of the car park. From its location, it was assumed to be the floor of the Corn Exchange. At the northern end of the site, concrete flooring surfaced with terrazzo could be seen, a survival from the twentieth-century public toilets which had been located in this area.

Many pits were revealed, mostly smaller than the midden or cellar pits already mentioned. One near the east end of the long stone wall was largely filled with cinders and another, just west of the fourth well had some colourful infill, containing the remains of burnt wattle and daub. It was in the topmost layer of this pit that the most interesting metal object was found, a medieval bronze buckle (63).

When the service road to the west of the new library was being prepared and laid in May 1987, it involved reducing the level of the surrounding land by a significant amount and this provided the opportunity for further archaeology. The conditions were even more difficult than during the 1986 campaign, given the cramped working space and the need for contractor's lorries to gain access over the same narrow piece of ground. Despite these constraints, a small excavation was opened down the extreme western edge of the site. Stripping of the residual tarmac had uncovered some stones in this area, close to the remnant of the adjacent boundary wall. They proved to be the capping of a drain running north–south, close to and parallel with, the western boundary (see plan, 49). This drain was followed northwards until it was cut, at right angles, by another wall. Beyond this again was a stone-flagged floor, back-filled with building rubble but still retaining a covering of coal dust (54). From its location, this structure was identifiable as the cellar of the Hall Keeper's House (48). This was once the home of Mr Henry Jesty, the Town Hall Keeper, Mace-bearer, Town Crier, Toll Collector and Bill Poster. He was a larger than life figure in Yeovil at the turn of the twentieth century. The Ham stone flags of Mr Jesty's cellar fitted together so precisely, that it was not possible to put a trowel between them. At the northern extremity of the cellar was a Ham stone step, still in situ and worn in the middle with use. This marked the entrance to the cellar from the end of the kitchen, which ran across the back of the house (this information was supplied by Mrs I. Taylor who had lived in the house as a girl). Another step had been observed as the overburden was removed by mechanical excavator.

South of the covered drain a stone wall ran east–west, parallel to South Street, possibly part of an earlier cottage fronting South Street. This wall cut a

54 Left 1987, west end of the cellar of the Hall Keeper's House. The front wall of the house cut an older drain (foreground) and the cellar still retained some coal. © *B. and M. Gittos*

55 Below Fragments of burnt daub with preserved imprints of the wattle, from one of the colourful pits on the Library Site. This is debris from a timber-framed building destroyed by fire. © *Alan Gittos*

pit which contained baked clay debris and charcoal from a burnt building. Another area, close to the new library wall, appeared to show at least two such pits cutting one another. The lower, i.e. earlier, of these yielded some pottery and part of a possibly late sixteenth-century clay pipe. These pits were of a similar nature to the colourful pit found in 1986 and in the same general area. At the north end of the site the massive foundations of the Town Hall were exposed. At one location, it was apparent that they were built over an earlier stone wall which was also parallel to the High Street. The other notable feature was the continuation of the cobbled roadway through the Victorian markets (seen in 1986). It was exactly aligned with the existing alleyway through to the High Street and was made up of very large lias setts, edged with drainage gullies. Just to the west of the roadway there was an unexplained brick relieving arch in the Town Hall foundations and this had cut another of the colourful pits. The pieces of burnt clay which were present were very large and clearly showed imprints of wattle *(55)*. One sherd of medieval pottery was associated with this material.

PETTERS HOUSE

While the examination of the Library Site was still in progress, clearance began for construction of Petters House, only a short distance to the south in Petters

56 Site clearance in Petters Way in 1987. The demolition of the former public toilet block is underway. Behind the mechanical digger is the Baptist church and beyond that the new library. © *B. and M. Gittos*

Way *(56)*. This was a new District Council building to house voluntary organisations and the Tourist Information Centre. Attention was then split between these two locations with the main focus turning towards Petters Way.

Watts' map of 1806 shows that the area was occupied by a large property, with a long garden backing onto orchards. This was South Street House, the residence of Dr P.A. Colmer at the turn of the twentieth century, which formerly stood next to No.80 South Street (now the Community Arts Centre), shown here in another of Leslie Brooke's drawings *(57)*. A narrow alleyway (now Petters Way) separated it from the Baptist chapel. The area to be investigated was roughly at the end of the garden. Over a two-month period from May to July 1987, numerous visits were made to record features and collect samples. Again the cooperation of the contractors and individual workmen was excellent. Public toilets were demolished, the tarmac stripped from the car park and a new service trench dug round the northern extremity of the plot. This cut through some brick walls, which formed a narrow cleft, largely filled with broken glass vessels. Extreme care was needed in investigating this solid mass of hazardous material, as it turned out to be a cache of medicine bottles. It would appear that it was a dump associated with Dr Colmer's practice. Only some representative material was collected.

57 No.79 South Street, the residence and Surgery of Dr Colmer in the late nineteenth and early twentieth century. The rubbish pits from the end of the garden behind the house produced most of the finds from the Petters House site. *Drawing by Leslie Brooke. © Marjorie Brooke*

Unlike the level situation of the Library Site, the ground at Petters Way rises sharply to the east. The section revealed by the service trench showed that the area around the toilet block had been levelled, masking the natural slope and producing a greater depth of archaeological material towards the west. The need to build the lowest level of Petters House into the hillside meant that the whole area had to be excavated. For the most part, there was a shallow deposit of disturbed material overlying clean, light clay. However, towards the northern edge of the site five pits were exposed. Pit 3 was a minor, shallow, feature containing a mostly rubble fill with some large pieces of green glass wine bottles but the other four were of two distinct types. Pits 1 and 5 contained mostly cinders and fragments of clay pipes. Adjoining them were companion deposits 2 and 4 which comprised mainly bones, pottery and glass. The most fruitful of these was pit 4 which contained a great deal of pottery.

THE FINDS

More than 1000 items were collected from the Library Site in 1986 alone, comprising 145 pieces of bone; 152 pieces of clay pipe; 59 shells; 79 fragments of glass; 67 bricks or brick fragments; 22 pieces of stone; 22 metal objects and 446 sherds of pottery. These finds were not evenly distributed, with some features contributing a large proportion of the total. The most productive feature was the midden pit from which 169 pottery sherds were recovered. Taken together with the 77 sherds of probably related material from the adjacent trench, this accounted for more than half the pottery. Many pieces of clay pipe came from the same small area but the largest group belonged to the cinder pit at the north end of the site. Bone was recovered from both these areas and a significant collection was also recovered from the drain below the market road. A broad date range was represented by the finds, from the medieval period to the present day, but the bulk of the pottery and pipes dated from the eighteenth century. The following is an overview of the material from both sites.

Pottery

Both sites produced significant quantities of pottery, with the bulk of it coming from the midden pit on the Library Site *(colour plate 9)* and pit 4 at Petters House. Many types of vessel were represented. Chamber pots were recognisable by their upright walls and narrow flat rims. Fragments from several chamber pots came from the midden pit. The best example was found close to the base of the pit in 26 pieces and after reconstruction proved to be almost complete *(colour plate 11)*. It had been coated in a yellowish-brown glaze, somewhat sketchily applied in places. It was quite well constructed with its handle neatly blended in and the walls of a consistent thickness. It had, however, been badly over-fired, turning the fabric almost black in places and making it very friable. The base is rather thin and contains a small hole, which has been produced by an impact from below, with a sharp instrument. The fragile nature of the base had allowed it to be punctured in this way, without the whole vessel shattering. This would have contributed to its ultimate preservation because, as it was no longer fit for purpose, it would have been discarded whole. From the way the sherds were arranged, it was clear that the chamber pot was then crushed by other rubbish, subsequently thrown into the pit.

The smallest vessels identified are ointment pots, one of which is the only intact pot discovered. At the other extreme there are some sizeable fragments of the large, open, bowls called pancheons, which would have found a multitude of uses in Yeovil's eighteenth-century kitchens. Perhaps the most interesting type represented is the chafing dish *(58)*. Pieces of at least three were found. It is believed that they were used for keeping food warm and might have even been used for gentle cooking. They consisted of a wide shallow pierced bowl, with distinctive lugs set round the rim, standing on a hollow pedestal base with an opening in the side. A separate dish of food could be placed on top, supported by the lugs and kept warm by air rising from a heat source, placed below in the hollow base. Chafing dishes would have been useful when the

58 Two chafing dish fragments (a hollow base and one of the lugs from the rim of the bowl) from the Library Site midden pit. © *Alan Gittos*

kitchen was far removed from the dining area (perhaps even in a separate building) or when all the courses of a meal were placed on the table together. The desire to keep food warm in this way can be seen as a measure of refinement in the culinary affairs of the establishment and perhaps a reflection of its status. Chafing dishes are not commonly found in archaeological contexts of this kind and the presence of several vessels is noteworthy. Perhaps this pit contained rubbish from one of the inns. A number of fragments of pots with handles known as porringers were also identified, together with small pieces of imported German mugs and wine flasks. Part of a tankard has '1/8' stamped above the handle, probably reflecting the measure it contained.

The pottery fabrics from the 1986 campaign have been examined by David Dawson (a specialist on West Country pottery). Redwares are predominant, mostly of the South Somerset/Donyatt type with just a few sherds from Holnest in North Dorset. The kilns at Donyatt, only about 15 miles west of Yeovil, dominated the local market over a protracted period. Several of the kiln sites have been excavated and the wares are well known. However, a significant proportion of the Yeovil material is untypical of what is generally found in the region and is probably from a very local source which may have even been the town itself. A feature of this local material is the fact that the glaze is more tenacious and less liable to flake off than is commonly observed with pottery from the Donyatt kilns, with the material from which it is made also being different. There is a significant proportion of this local ware amongst the contents of the midden pit, including the chamber pot.

Much of the white ware is of nineteenth-century date, with only eight sherds of the earlier, more prestigious, tin-glazed Delft ware. Although originally made in Holland, many factories were set up to produce this material in Britain during the seventeenth century, notably in London and Bristol and production continued until the later eighteenth. There was even a short-lived enterprise at Wincanton (between *c*.1730 and 1750). This could have supplied

Yeovil but there is no easy way of recognising its products. A single piece of a tankard of Bristol 'mottled' ware is amongst the finds from the cinder pit. The distinctive Bristol yellow slipware, with its cream and brown slip decoration, is represented by some dozen sherds, including examples from the midden pit, datable to the early eighteenth century *(colour plate 14)*. The examples of salt-glazed stonewares which were found divide equally between sources in England and Germany, with the latter including five sherds of Westerwald and some pieces of Bellarmine bottles. An unusual item is half a relatively thick pot base of North Devon gritty ware. It had not been produced from the usual Fremington clay and despite its distinctive fabric is not closely datable. The very distinctive, and high quality Agate ware is represented on the Library Site by a single sherd, its marbled appearance being produced by mixing together differently coloured clays.

The pottery from pit 4 at Petters House includes substantial portions of two dishes of sgraffito slipware of the type produced by the potters at Donyatt. They have amber coloured glaze with the addition of green splashes scattered across them. The patterns are related and the larger dish sports a bold floral design of tulips *(colour plate 10)*. The central flower is shown in profile and the two to either side in plan. It has a double beaded rim, frilled with the thumb and a border of swags and dashes. The whole character of this dish closely resembles one which is in the collection of the Somerset County Museum (excavated from a Donyatt kiln site) and which currently forms the centrepiece of a display. This has a centrally placed cockerel surrounded by flowers, with a similar rim and is datable to about 1725. Many pieces of Bristol yellow slipware were found. Parts of two cups of this style survive, showing their full section and one of these retains its handle *(colour plate 12)*. Compared to what had just been found on the Library Site, there was a higher proportion of the more expensive products such as Delft *(colour plate 13)*. Several examples of hand painted porcelain (which would have come from China in the eighteenth century) were recovered and this was not a feature of the Library Site pits. All this evidence points to the fact that the household responsible for depositing the rubbish at Petters House was of a higher social order. It was to be expected that there would be differences in the character of the materials from the two sites because the pits at Petters House contained refuse from a single domestic property, whereas the Library Site covered a wide range of commercial and domestic activities.

Medieval pottery was collected from a number of locations across both sites. At Petters House, this appeared to be just a scatter of residual pieces, perhaps of thirteenth or fourteenth-century date. On the Library Site, there were about a dozen sherds of similar pottery, almost all of which were associated with the colourful pits.

4 Camouflage of the south wall of the old Gaumont Cinema (Top Ten Bingo Club) on the corner of South Street and Stars Lane. *Photo Jack W. Sweet*

5 The baluster shown in *colour plate 3* as it was discovered. © *B. and M. Gittos*

6 Above The church of St Mary the Virgin, Stoke sub Hamdon remains, despite later alterations, an essentially Norman building. © *B. and M. Gittos*

7 Left Norman corbel carved with a running hare. Part of the corbel table on the south side of the chancel at St Mary's Stoke sub Hamdon. © *B. and M. Gittos*

8 Opposite Memorial window in St Mary's church to Dr Richard Hensleigh Walter FSA who died in 1924. Physician and archaeologist, he was the last of three generations of the Walter family to study the archaeology of the area. © *B. and M. Gittos*

9 Below A collection of material from the midden pit including sherds of Westerwald, Delft ware, Donyatt and probable Yeovil-made pottery. © *Alan Gittos*

10 Left Large broken dish from pit 4, Petters House. This is a typical Donyatt product and dates from *c.*1725. © *B. and M. Gittos*

11 Above left Chamber pot from the Library Site midden pit. Although badly broken it was almost complete. Probably a local imitation of Donyatt products. © *Alan Gittos*

12 Above right Section of a Bristol yellow slipware cup from pit 4, Petters House. © *B. and M. Gittos*

13 Right, above Two sherds of a Delft ware bowl from the Library Site midden pit. © *Alan Gittos*

14 Right, below Samples of Library Site pottery including Bristol yellow slipware (top and right) and Donyatt (left). © *Alan Gittos*

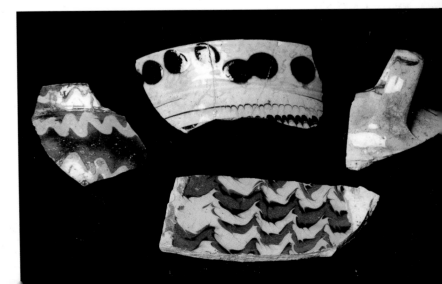

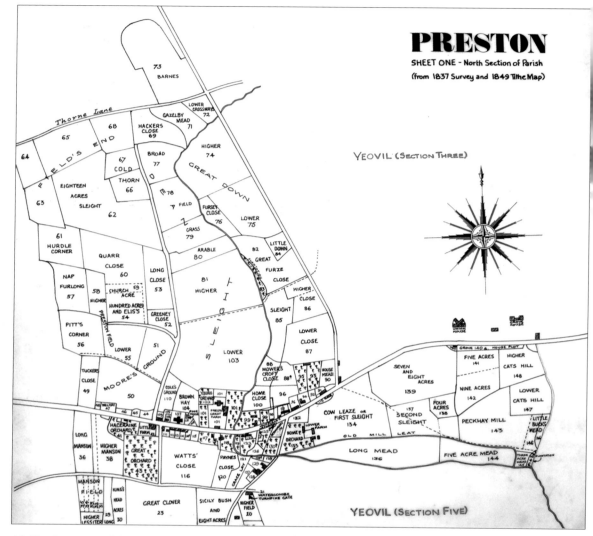

15 Northern area of the Preston Tithe map (1849) redrawn by Leslie Brooke who added the field names from the 1837 survey. © *Marjorie Brooke*

59 A typical eighteenth-century clay pipe bowl from Petters House. There were approximately 300 fragments of pipe recovered from the two sites.
© B. and M. Gittos

Clay Pipes

Approximately 300 pieces of clay pipe were found on the two sites, including many complete bowls but makers' stamps were unfortunately rare. A typical eighteenth-century example from Petters Way is shown in *59*. Two bowls embossed with a letter P set within a circle were found in the midden pit but are not readily identifiable. Very similar pipes were found during the Donyatt kiln excavations, datable to between about 1690 and 1730. Three pipes from Petters House have 'WN' beneath ★, placed low on the back of the bowl. These were probably produced by one of two eighteenth-century Bristol pipe makers, William Naylor or William Nicholas. Another pipe bears the name John Pitcher on its base and a pipe of this maker is known from Taunton and dated around 1650. Three Petters House pipes have 'ID' marked on their bases and makers with these initials have been recorded from both Bath and Bristol. However pipes with this identity have been found from many locations in the town and a local origin for them must be a possibility. Despite the paucity of identifiable sources for the pipes, from the form of the bowls it is clear that the great majority date from the eighteenth century with only a few examples being earlier. One of these was found in association with the footings of the long wall on the Library Site. Only a single case of a nineteenth-century bowl with fluted decoration was discovered. One of the pipe bowls from the midden pit has finger prints preserved on it in orange paint, presumably evidence of an eighteenth-century Yeovil decorator!

Bone

Many of the pieces of bone from the Library Site are small and not easy to identify. Of those which are, the most notable are part of the lower jaw of a pig, a cow's incisor and the skull of a rabbit. Some of the bones show signs of butchery *(60)*, the more obvious of which came from the brick-lined drain presumably from where it ran past the Meat Market. Other bones with knife

marks were found in the more domestic contexts, such as the midden and cinder pits. Probably the most significant of the organic remains is a horn core *(61)*. This is the light structure which supports a horn and attaches it to the skull. The piece recovered comprises a large portion of core together with a small section of skull. The core shows clear evidence of cut marks where the horn has been stripped away. The horn itself was extremely valuable for making many items such as buttons, combs and cups. Horn cores are commonly found on both horn-working and leather-dressing sites, the two industries being closely related. The bones recovered from Petters House tend to be larger than those from the Library Site but without obvious signs of butchery although, again, knife marks are sometimes present.

Shell

Oyster shells were found widely scattered across both sites but without any particular concentrations and there was a tendency for them to accumulate on contractor's spoil heaps. The nine fragments from the cinder pit on the Library Site proved to be the largest group. Six snail shells came from the fill of the roadway drain and a single scallop shell was found near the old library wall. It is surprising that more oyster shells were not found amongst deposits such as the midden pit.

Glass

Most of the glass is derived from wine bottles. Many fragments of these dumpy, dark green, onion-shaped bottles were recovered from both locations but the largest and most complete examples, dating from the eighteenth century, came from pit 3 at Petters House. On the Library Site only a single neck was recovered, with bases predominating. A chance find was made by the site agent. It is a large portion of a handmade drinking glass, which is probably of eighteenth-century date *(62)*. The items recovered from Dr Colmer's medicine

60 Opposite, left Some examples of animal bones exhibiting marks of butchery, from the Library Site, and likely to have been associated with the meat market. © *Alan Gittos*

61 Opposite, right Part of a horn core from the Library Site. This would have been left over after removal of the horn itself for making a wide range of products, e.g. buttons, combs or glue. © *Alan Gittos*

62 Right The lower part of an eighteenth-century drinking glass, found on the Library Site. © *Alan Gittos*

bottle cache at Petters House include two largely intact bottles which have teaspoon graduations moulded into the glass and a third is similarly graduated, in tablespoons. There are some fragmentary measuring cylinders but other complete items include three small clear-glass phials and a ground-glass stopper.

Small Finds

There were few small finds and no coins. This may have been due to the way in which the watching brief had to be carried out. In a conventional excavation, the investigator removes the earth and is in a position to examine it for finds. However, on confined building sites the contractor rapidly removes the spoil by lorry and no further examination of the excavated material is possible. This was the case at both locations and recording was therefore mostly limited to what was visible in the sections created by the contractor's trenches. Even allowing for these restrictions, the complete absence of coins is difficult to explain. This is also true of many other plots examined in the town and, perhaps, the conclusion is that Yeovilians have always been very careful with their money!

The most important metal object found is the bronze buckle from the colourful pit examined in 1986. It is of spectacle form with its tang still free to operate *(63)*. Both the straight sides are decorated with simple incised chevrons, three on one side and four on the other. Incised dashes can still be traced across

63 Left Fifteenth-century bronze buckle from one of the colourful pits on the Library Site. © *Alan Gittos*

64 Opposite Fragment of a ridge tile from a post-medieval roof, with scalloped cresting and sparingly-applied green glaze. © *Alan Gittos*

one end. Retained within these decorations, are remnants of a coating, possible of tin. This would have given the buckle a silvery appearance when it was new. From comparison with published examples, it probably dates from early in the fifteenth century. The only other small find of note is the little domino from the fill of the drain in front of the Hall Keeper's House. It had been well carved from bone but there was no sign of its fellows.

Building Materials

A variety of building materials was apparent on the Library Site. Ham stone was found in different areas: blocks were present in the long stone wall and it was also used for a rain runnel, drain capping and the top of the third well. Lias occurred in the setts of the roadway and a doorstep. Brick was widely distributed, the older examples being handmade. One of these, almost a cube in shape, had apparently been part of a hearth or fireplace and others had been used in the construction of wells and the long drain. The well bricks had been manufactured for the purpose, being keystone shaped. All these handmade bricks are likely to be of local manufacture as several brick makers are known to have worked in the town and part of St Michael's Avenue was formerly named Brickyard Lane (see Chapter 6). Perhaps the most interesting item of building material is a portion of ridge tile, with green-glaze sparingly applied to its scalloped crest *(64)*. Such tiles were used from medieval times but this example is post-medieval.

Burnt Material

The finds from the colourful pits should be considered as a whole. The first example was located near the South Street end of the Library Site, at the

western limit of the area uncovered in 1986 and close to the fourth well. Its fill was streaked with red and black from burnt debris, much of which had reverted back to the clay from which it was originally derived. Some samples of this fill were recovered and proved to be shapeless lumps of clay which had been fired or burnt. They contained many holes, the spaces left by the straw which had formed part of the composition. Better preserved material from the north end of the site showed clear evidence of wattle imprints *(55)*. This provides an explanation for the colourful pits. The material is building debris, the remains of timber-framed buildings with wattle and daub walls which had been destroyed by fire. Significantly, some later medieval pottery and the bronze buckle are associated with these deposits.

CONCLUSIONS

The activities of 1986/7 were undertaken in difficult conditions without expert knowledge of how to tackle such a complex urban site. Many points of detail which would have been apparent to the professional archaeologist were probably missed. Nevertheless, if nothing had been attempted the evidence would simply have been lost and, as it turned out, a great deal of useful information was obtained. The evidence completely refuted the deep scepticism which had previously prevailed in the town about the possibility of Yeovil having any surviving archaeology. Because so little work of this kind had previously been attempted in the town, it was not surprising that some of the findings would prove significant. The strong indication of an unrecorded local redware pottery source, was one such example. There is ample evidence that bricks were manufactured in the town, as explained in Chapter 6. Since the making of bricks and pottery both depend on the availability of suitable clays and comparable technology, the local manufacture of redware pots is credible. A number of clay pipes from Petters House bore the maker's stamp 'ID'. Similar pipes have been found elsewhere in the town and perhaps they too were made locally, using imported clays. Nothing is currently known about such enterprises in Yeovil and here is a case of archaeology asking questions for historians to answer. Without doubt, the YALHS watching briefs at the library and Petters House in 1986/7 were a considerable success and still remain the most extensive archaeological recording to have been carried out in Yeovil.

The discovery of considerable quantities of burnt wattle and daub in several different areas was particularly interesting, given the number of times Yeovil is known to have been afflicted by fires. There is now recognition that debris from such events, dating back at least to the fifteenth century still remains in the town. Given the relationship of the area under scrutiny to the heart of the medieval settlement as represented by the Borough, it was disappointing that no material which could be dated earlier than about 1400 was uncovered. This might have been due to the limited depth of the foundation trenches and the random way in which the archaeological features were being exposed.

The scatter of medieval pot sherds found across the Petters House site was not associated with any particular medieval features and the older maps simply show orchards in this area. However, they could be indicative of medieval occupation in this part of the town, and this supports a growing impression that the medieval borough may be on a different axis from the east–west alignment of the later town. A number of archaeological observations in Middle Street have failed to find any archaeological deposits at all, suggesting that much of the eastern spread of the town may have occurred in post-medieval times. Perhaps the axis of the medieval borough was north–south in the direction of the adjacent manors of Kingston and Hendford. Only more archaeology will provide the answers.

CHAPTER 6

YEOVIL'S HISTORY THROUGH MAPS

Duncan Black

INTRODUCTION

In this chapter, the story of Yeovil will be studied by means of maps, against a backdrop of the known history of the town over the past 200 years. Some 20 maps have been used. They are of varying quality and date and were produced by a variety of sources, for different purposes. Perhaps the best known to readers, will be those produced by the Ordnance Survey. About one third of the maps used in the study come from this source. The earliest of these which is of a useful scale, is the 1886 large scale map of 1:500 or, about 120in to the mile. This is a good example of the cartographer's art, drawn in stunning detail *(65)*. Post Office letter boxes, lamp posts and even the landscaping detail of some of the gardens of the grander houses are all shown. The modern digital equivalent, although possibly slightly more accurate, is but a pale shadow of these older maps. Another group of maps was produced for official purposes, such as the Tithe map of 1842 (drawn to ensure that the tithes were properly administered) and two maps commissioned by the Yeovil town authorities, the Estate Map of 1813 and the Borough Drainage Map of 1858. However, only the 1842 map is considered here. The remaining maps were all produced for commercial purposes. They vary enormously in date, scale and accuracy, covering different areas of the town and its surroundings. The majority of them date from the nineteenth and twentieth centuries, although the earliest was drawn in the seventeenth century. This is Philip Byles' map of Lyde, 1653, reproduced as one of the end papers of *The Book of Yeovil*.

There are some inherent difficulties with studies such as this. The techniques of modern map-making were not practised until the sixteenth century and this necessarily limits the period which can be studied. Another problem is that by the time a map has been drawn, it is usually out of date, and is

65 Part of the 1886 Ordnance Survey showing the town centre between Middle Street and Vicarage Street, redrawn by Leslie Brooke. © *Marjorie Brooke*

essentially a historical document. It is often the case that maps drawn at about the same time will show different degrees of detail, even allowing for matters of scale. This may be a consequence of the purposes for which the map was produced or the skill of the map maker. So essentially, a study through maps can be seen as viewing a series of idiosyncratic snapshots in time. Nevertheless, such a study can reveal much detail of the development of an area, in a manner not achievable using other methods.

HISTORICAL BACKGROUND

Nineteenth century

Given the available material what follows will concentrate on the story of the development of Yeovil from the early nineteenth century but before analysing what the maps tell us, it is important to establish the principal elements of the town's historical development since 1800. At this time it was a small market town making textiles and gloves, with a brick industry largely geared to local demand. Subsequently, Yeovil evolved into a centre for making some 90 per cent of the nation's gloves and, finally, when all these industries had long gone, the manufacture of helicopters and associated advanced technologies. A small part of the leather industry survives, but even this has moved on and Pittards is now a world leader in leather technology.

At the beginning of the nineteenth century, although Yeovil was a fairly large parish, it had no separate legal status as a town (for the origins of the town, see Chapter 3). The population in the 1801 census was 2774. The area was rural, with 20 farms within the parish. The town provided the market services for the surrounding area, of both south Somerset and north Dorset. Apart from the normal agricultural products at the weekly market, there was also a considerable trade in flax and hemp, satisfying demand from the local textile industry. This business waned, but trade in sheep remained buoyant. A large number of animal pens is identified on the nineteenth-century maps. The scale of the trade is implied by the fact that they are all sheep pens. Growth of the town is demonstrated by the fact that in 1853 it had approximately 1700 houses.

By the late 1820s the need for improved local government in the town resulted in a Parliamentary Bill, entitled *An Act for paving, lighting, watching, watering, cleansing, repairing and widening and otherwise improving the streets, lanes and other public passages and places within the town of Yeovil and for regulating the Police thereof.* It received the Royal Assent in June 1830. One of the results of this Act, was to extend the town boundary, within the parish. This and the later extensions are shown in *66* and *67*. A further boundary extension was made in 1854, when, also by Act of Parliament, Yeovil was established as a Municipal Borough in its own right. By the 1861 census, the population had risen to 8486. Up until the late nineteenth century, there had been a somewhat confusing situation of the borough acting as a separate entity within the large parish of Yeovil. This was resolved in 1894, when the area outside the 1854 boundary was renamed 'Yeovil Without', which still exists although reduced in area, as the result of the expanding town. A further boundary extension took place in 1904, when part of Preston Plucknett parish was absorbed, and again in 1928 when a further part of Preston Plucknett was subsumed, together with a tiny portion of East Coker. Today the settlement of Yeovil continues to expand, and it has now completely outgrown the boundary established in 1928, especially to the west and south.

In the middle of the nineteenth century, there was a brief time of recession in the town and the arrival of the railways provided a great boost to local industry, the ease of distribution facilitating significant growth, particularly in the dairying and gloving trades. At its peak over 400,000 pairs of gloves were manufactured in a single year. Raw materials for their manufacture could now be readily imported from far and wide. Rail access also meant that other raw

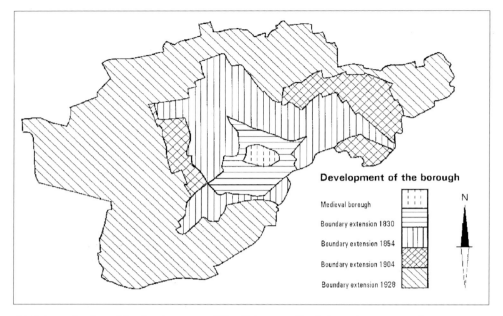

Development of the borough

Medieval borough

Boundary extension 1830

Boundary extension 1854

Boundary extension 1904

Boundary extension 1928

N

66 Schematic plan of the development of Yeovil since medieval times, in summary form.
© *Duncan Black*

materials such as coal could easily be brought in, to meet the needs of both domestic and industrial customers. Considerable quantities of coal would have been required, not only for the new gas industry but also by the Yeovil Iron and Brass Foundry and the Nautilus Grate Works in Hendford. Importation of coal, using the poor roads of the time, presented a limitation to the expansion of industry. Whilst benefiting industry, the railways inevitably caused the decline and eventual abandonment of the long distance coach routes, with the consequent effect on the coaching inns in the town. However, the local carriage trade of both passengers and goods would continue to be horse drawn for at least a further 50 years. Even before the motor car arrived, traffic problems were being encountered, especially in the centre of town, where the medieval street plan was still extant. The introduction of motor vehicles was gradual and it would be some thirty years before any significant effects would be felt. One casualty of the rise of the motor car was the long established firm of carriage builders, Hill and Boll, who had large works in Kingston and Park Road.

By the end of the nineteenth century, the gloving industry was already in slow decline, which continued until the closure of the last glove factory in 1989. Many former glove factories have survived adapted to other purposes, such as this splendid example in the former Waterloo Lane *(68)*. As the manufacture of gloves reduced, two new industries had emerged, both having their roots in agriculture and both of them growing to be enterprises of national prominence. They were the dairy produce firm, best known by its trade name

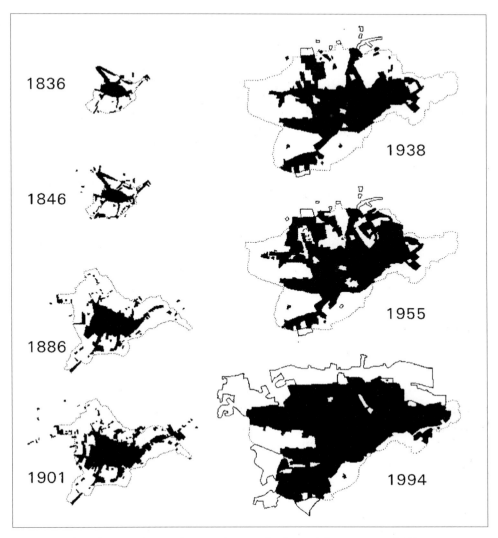

67 Series of developmental maps showing the growth of Yeovil from 1836 until 1994.
© *Duncan Black*

1836 1830 town boundary shown dotted. Medieval town outline still discernable but with
      Kingston and Upper Kingston well developed.
1846 1830 boundary dotted. Although medieval town outline still discernable, scatters of
      development now evident.
1886 1854 Borough boundary dotted. Medieval town outline now lost. General growth
      around town core and considerable scatter elsewhere.
1901 1854 Borough boundary dotted. General increase in development.
1938 General growth but little outside borough boundary.★
1955 Limited development, prior to post-war boom.★
1994 Considerable development, much well beyond the former borough boundary.★

★1938, 1955 & 1994. Dotted lines show 1928 borough boundary, solid lines are limit of
development outside this.

68 Waterloo House, a former gloving factory now used as office premises in Waterloo Avenue (originally Lane). © *B. and M. Gittos*

of St Ivel and the other, the helicopter manufacturer Westland. In the 1880s Aplin and Barrett were described as cheese factors. In 1897 they became known as Western Counties Creameries and, at about the same time, moved to a new, larger, site in Newton Road. In 1901 they adopted the brand name of St Ivel. In 1868 James Petter acquired an established ironmongery business in the Borough, later moving into manufacturing. The firm of Petter and Edgar was responsible for some notable inventions, including the Nautilus fire grate, which achieved nationwide recognition and royal patronage. From this they progressed to the manufacture of a very successful range of stationary oil engines, establishing their reputation in the engineering field.

Twentieth century

Following the outbreak of the First World War, Petters began the manufacture of aircraft under licence in 1915 at their new factory, which they had recently established to the west of the town. As well as the purchase of land for their new factory, an additional plot was acquired to build a garden village to accommodate their workforce, centred on Westland Road. During the war they used their other factory, the Nautilus Works in Reckleford, to make munitions. The name of the aircraft manufacturing business was changed to Westland Aircraft Ltd, which became known worldwide. In 1916 they achieved the historic distinction of having built the first aircraft to take part in a naval battle, when their fourth licence-built Short 184 took part in the battle of Jutland. The remains of this aircraft, which belong to the Imperial War Museum, are on display nearby at the Fleet Air Arm Museum. The association with the building of aircraft for the Royal Navy has continued to the present day. Although Westland originally built seaplanes, they soon began landplane construction.

The first airfield, which is the eastern part of the present site, opened in April 1917 with its western boundary marked by the original course of Watercombe Lane. The factory was located on the south side of the airfield, alongside the Yeovil to Durston railway line, with its own private sidings. The bridge which took Watercombe Lane over this railway line still stands near the western entrance to the Westland site. As aircraft performance increased, they required greater take off and landing distances and the runway had to be extended. This was achieved by diverting the centre part of Watercombe Lane. Westland survived the post-war dip in demand for aircraft and when Britain began to rearm in the later half of the 1930s they were well placed to benefit from the upturn. The factory therefore expanded to meet this demand. This assured Yeovil of its continuing prosperity, as by now, Westland was the largest employer in the town.

Although, perhaps, not considered significant at the time, the factory occupied a large area, which would have been ideal for residential development and without it, the development of the town might have followed a very different pattern. The shape of Yeovil was already causing comment in town planning circles, due to ribbon development taking place along the principle roads leading out of the town. This had generally reached the limits of the borough boundary. By the early 1930s there had been a considerable change in this situation with infilling both to the west and in the east. Further housing development was to follow, particularly to the north and south-west. During the 1930s, road traffic began to be seen as a real problem and the possibility of bypassing the centre was considered and at least part of the proposed line was protected in planning terms and this can still be identified on later maps by the unusually wide verges. Parts of Larkhill Road, Preston Road and Watercombe Lane are the best examples of this in the town.

Yeovil had been involved in the human aspects of the First World War when, for example, the local British Red Cross Society established a 62 bed hospital in the town, which by the end of the war had treated some 1200 casualties. However, the Second World War brought conflict to Yeovil itself, for the first time, when the town suffered ten air raids. During these raids, nearly 3000 houses were damaged, representing about one third of the town's housing stock. For the surviving reminders of the Second World War, see Chapter 7. After the war the town can be said to have blossomed, both in terms of housing and of industry. To the east and west of the town new commercial complexes have been established, although some of these lie partly outside the town boundary. The activities carried on within these areas cover manufacturing, service industries and retailing. The town continues to expand.

Housing

In the middle of the nineteenth century, there were serious concerns about the state of public health in the town and an enquiry was held. When it was published in 1852, the Rammell Report was extremely critical of the poor housing, inadequate sanitation and bad water quality (there were still open sewers in parts of the town, and in numerous cases, wells had been sunk adjacent to privy shafts). Dr William Tomkins, a Town Commissioner who gave evidence to the Rammell Enquiry, described Yeovil in 1849 as 'a very filthy, a very dirty and a very stinking place'. The scandalous picture presented by the report was an important factor in ensuring that, two years later, the town finally gained the status and administration of a borough. The report illuminated the great disparity between the living conditions of the wealthy and the lowest paid. Many of the more modest houses were described as 'haunts of disease'. After the creation of the borough the worst of the old housing was removed and the building of modern Yeovil began.

The first 150 municipal houses were built at New Town, just prior to the First World War, 'to meet the needs of the working classes'. Between the wars, a total of 1600 houses was built. In 1946, the first phase of municipal building in the post-war era, saw the establishment of an estate of 150 prefabricated bungalows, on and to the west of Larkhill Road. The roads to serve the houses to the west of Larkhill Road were built by Italian prisoners of war and a small length of their concrete construction can still be found today. These prefabricated houses were followed over the next few years, by some 700 conventional examples. Those which were built in the early post-war period were situated around the newly opened western part of Stiby Road. The eastern part of Stiby Road had formerly been known as Lower Larkhill Lane. In the east of the town, the developments at this time were in Tower, Milford and Greenhill Roads, and also in Elmhurst, Chelston and St Georges Avenues. Subsequently, municipal housing gave way to private development, to meet the needs of an increasingly prosperous and homeowning population. This has continued to the present time, mainly to the north and west of the town and now well outside the 1928 boundary. There has however, been some infilling, particularly on former industrial sites, such as glove factories. Some housing was lost with the relocation of the District Hospital in the late 1960s. A considerably larger number disappeared when Yeovil's first major traffic alleviation scheme was introduced. This was the Queensway (Inner Relief Road Scheme) of the early 1970s. More recently, the construction of the Quedam shopping complex in the early 1980s caused further losses, involving Vicarage Street, Vincent Street and Earle Street.

This then, is an outline of Yeovil's nineteenth and twentieth-century past. The descriptions of the maps which follow will attempt to show how a study of maps can illuminate and enhance that history. Inevitably, the maps which are available fall short of the ideal, in terms of the information which they could provide but the results are, nevertheless, rewarding.

THE MAPS

Watts map, 1806

The earliest useful map showing a reasonable area of Yeovil, is that of 1806, which was surveyed by E. Watts *(69)*. A very prominent feature of this map, is the sheer number of orchards shown. They surround the town on every side. Next, one notices how clearly it shows the town to be centred on the parish church of St John the Baptist and this underpins the arguments set out in Chapter 3, for the importance of the church in the origins of the town. Then one notices some unfamiliar street names. London Road is obviously the Sherborne Road of today, but some mental adjustment is necessary to recognise that Ryalls Lane, a minor feature in the top right-hand corner of the map, is now Eastland Road. Cattle Market and Sheep Lane are more familiar today as Princes Street and North Lane respectively. Then it can be seen that some street names appear to have moved. Market Street was then known as Reckleford, whilst the Reckleford of today is called Reckleford Hill and has a wayside cross marked in the road close to the junction with the modern Market Street. West Hendford was then known as Salthouse Lane and the

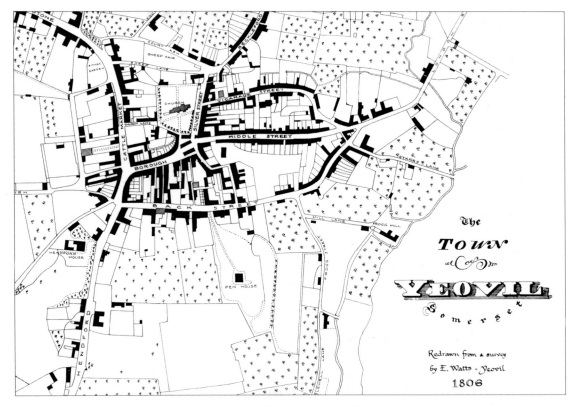

69 Watts map of 1806, beautifully redrawn by Leslie Brooke. © *Marjorie Brooke*

YEOVIL: THE HIDDEN HISTORY

Salthouse Lane of today is shown as Horses Lane. In 1806 South Street was called Back Street but later reverted to its original name. Frogg Street and Addlewell Lane described a large semi-circle from Back Street all the way to near the bottom of Hendford Hill. Although unnamed on the map, minor streets are shown including Wine Street, George Court, Red Lion Lane and Tabernacle Lane. The loss of George Court in 1928 has been described in Chapter 5. Red Lion Lane is now underneath the District Hospital. Tabernacle Lane still exists, although it was previously called Narrow Lane, Little Lane and later in the nineteenth century was also frequently referred to as Hannam's Lane. The Calvinistic Tabernacle chapel, from which the lane took its name, was itself demolished in 1971.

Buildings are not generally named on the map, exceptions being Hendford House, Pen House and Frogg Mill. Surprisingly, Frogg Mill did not stand on Frogg Street, but at the eastern end of Mill Lane. Some features are also named. Firstly, there is a brickyard on the south side of Lower Kingston, just north of what is now the Conservative Club (the former Duke of York public house). Pitney Gardens are shown occupying a triangle at the northern end of Cattle Market, opposite Sheep Lane and what is now the Court Ash car park, is labelled 'Sheep Fair'. Although unnamed, five religious buildings other than St John's can be identified, in Back Street, Cattle Market, Lower Kingston, Vicarage Street and Tabernacle Lane. They are shown cross-hatched to distinguish them from other buildings which are solid shapes. None of these have survived to the present time, although the first two have been replaced by more modern buildings. The development in Middle Street does not extend below the area of about the present Glovers Walk. The main area of occupation at this time, can be seen to be bounded by Higher Kingston, Reckleford Hill, Reckleford, Vicarage Street, Middle Street, Back Street, Cattle Market and Lower Kingston. Outside this area there are only scattered individual buildings, whilst even within the area there is much open space. The population at this time would have been approximately 2700.

The drainage of the central area is shown as a small stream flowing from west to east, roughly along the line of Central Road. This was known as the Rackel stream, with another small unnamed stream flowing from north to south just west of Eastland Road. These streams merged in the region of South Western Terrace, before flowing south to enter Dodham Brook behind the modern entertainment centre, on the site of the old Town Station. Although both the smaller streams have long since disappeared, Dodham Brook still effectively delineates the expansion of Yeovil in that area.

Day map, 1831

The Day map of 1831 was drawn up soon after the town boundary had been extended in 1830. It is somewhat less detailed than the 1806 map, but nevertheless, it is an important part of the story. On this map, Penn Hill, The Park,

Belmont, Bond and Brunswick Streets have appeared, as has the New Cut, now Wyndham Street. Ryalls Lane has become Kiddle's Lane, Goldcroft Lane has become Milford Lane, whilst the part of Back Street from Bond Street to Hendford has become South Street. The present West Hendford, which had been known as Salthouse Lane in 1806, is marked as Horses Lane. Paralleling the modern Salthouse Lane, a new street has appeared, named Willington Street, although that is clearly a misprint for Wellington Street. The western end of Addlewell Lane has become Chants Path. No buildings are named on this map, although some structures of industrial scale are now being shown. There is evidence of infilling in the area between Princes Street and Clarence Street, particularly at the southern end. There are also some larger buildings on the western side of Clarence Street and two more have appeared south of Addlewell Lane. The new Belmont and Park Streets have almost continuous terraced housing on the Penn Hill side only. On the northern side of Middle Street the development reaches almost to its eastern extremity. On the south side of London Road opposite the triangle formed with Wyndham Street and Reckleford there are both residential and industrial buildings. There is also some development in the lower part of Hendford and Brunswick Street.

Madeley map, 1831
Also in 1831, a detailed plan of Yeovil parish was produced by G.E. Madeley. It shows the field layout, roads, rivers and farms but does not deal with the buildings in Yeovil itself. It is of very similar form to the Yeovil Tithe map (see below), with all the fields individually numbered albeit to a different system. Even by this date, only small patches of medieval strip fields survived, the best example being three fields linked by a trackway where Westland's airfield is now located. These can be identified (using the Tithe map) as Higher, Middle and Lower Northover, all that remained of the North Field of Hendford Manor. It was over this rural landscape that Yeovil would expand, during the next 170 years or so. Some of these field boundaries have survived and can still be identified today, despite the housing developments which now envelope them. Examples of this will be mentioned later.

Tithe map, 1842
The Yeovil Tithe map of 1842 preserved in the County Record Office, was compiled for a different purpose than the other maps discussed here. It was produced to identify the ownership of land and property so that this information could be used in the collection of monies due (i.e. the tithes) from owners and tenants. The map itself is at first something of a disappointment. It is not drawn to a particularly high standard and displays minimal detail in terms of its lack of road names and only identifying a few key properties such as Pen House, Hendford House, Kingston Manor House and Hollands. However, its great value lies with the accompanying explanatory document known as the

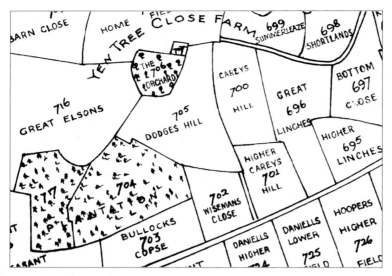

70 A section of the 1842 Tithe map showing fields around Yew Tree Close Farm. Redrawn by Leslie Brooke with the field names from the Tithe Apportionment added. © *Marjorie Brooke*

'Tithe Apportionment', dated four years later (1846). This is a list of the property and/or land held by each owner, with every item being identified by a unique reference number and shown as such on the map. It is a simple list just acting as an index to the map but it contains a wealth of information in the column entitled 'Name and Description of Lands and Premises'. In many cases this is just a field name, e.g. Pennys Mead, New Pound and Tuckers Mead all owned by John Batten. However, within the town itself, the descriptions can be more informative. Plot 493 is described as 'Gas Works and Garden' and is shown next to the area, on the south side of London Road, which had previously been the Workhouse but was now owned by James Whitby. Two otherwise anonymous buildings in Frogg Street on plots 460 and 461 both appear in the list as 'Gloving Yard and Gardens'. Plot 111 in Vicarage Street, on the other hand, is not surprisingly identified as the Vicarage. In this case further useful information is provided because, whilst the owner is stated to be Revd Robert Phelips (Vicar of St John's 1815-55), it was occupied by the Revd William Robinson. These are only a few examples of the enormous value of the Tithe map in adding to our knowledge of nineteenth-century Yeovil. Its other great strength is the richness of information it contains regarding field names and local place names. Often field names provide the only clues to hidden history. To illustrate this from the Yeovil map there are three field names which include the word 'quarry'. Plot 1070 (Quarry Field) was situated just north of Hollands, within the campus of Yeovil College; plot 1357 (Quarry Ground) was close to Brimsmore Farm and finally plot 953 (also Quarry Ground) is now in a built up area of the town, beside St Michael's Avenue and just to the south of Bucklers Mead School. Undoubtedly, quarrying of local stone played a significant part in Yeovil's past but very little is known about the industry and the Tithe map provides some clues. A small section of the Tithe map around Yew Tree Close Farm is shown in *(70)* and part of the Preston map can be seen in *(colour plate 15)*. Another version of the Tithe map was drawn by W. Bidder of Yeovil in 1843 and has been published as one of the endpapers of *The Book of Yeovil*.

Ordnance Survey, 1886

Undoubtedly, the 1886 map (scale 1:500) is the best such representation of Yeovil's past that we have *(65)*. It shows the borough, when the population was about 9500. The town was already a centre for the treatment of leather and gloving, having been involved in glove making since medieval times. Twelve glove factories are shown, most of them being relatively small, but one large example was on the north side of Middle Street. This was the premises of the Whitby brothers and Glovers Walk perpetuates the memory of this important gloving company. Another part of the gloving industry, the preparation of the leather, was shown by the presence of numerous large dressing yards. One such was situated on the western side of Kiddle's Lane, now Eastland Road. The name Kiddles still survives as a small housing estate in this area. Other large dressing yards were situated in Addlewell Lane, with two in Brunswick Street, the latter in the area of the Goldenstones Leisure Centre. Near here was a Patent Twine Works. One dressing yard is already shown as disused. It lay to the north of Preston Road, immediately west of the cemetery. There was also a leather factory in lower Middle Street, which was acquired by the Pittard family in 1848 and which still stands, set back on the north side, just east of the junction with Central Road. There was a considerable brick-making industry in Yeovil, mostly situated on the northern side of the town. The Yeovil Brick Works was at the bottom of Goldcroft, then known as Goldcroft Lane, on the eastern side and extending almost to Kiddle's Lane. This was a self contained industry using the clay from a pit within the site *(71)*. The remains of a brick-making kiln are also shown in the centre of New Town near the Primitive Methodist Chapel. This latter building is now used by Jehovah's Witnesses. It is likely that many of the earlier houses still standing in the town were built with local Yeovil bricks.

There were other industries in the town, perhaps the best known name being that of the Nautilus Grate factory near the top of Hendford on the eastern side. This was the only Nautilus Works shown, as the better-known premises in Reckleford had not then been built. The other metal working site in the town was the Yeovil Iron and Brass Foundry, which was in Clarence Street. This was Petter's first engineering works and, in turn, the forerunner of Westland. The site now lies under Tesco's car park. At the top of Addlewell Lane, there was a shirt and collar factory, this being, of course, the era of the detached collar! In terms of the 1886 map, this factory seems to be the only surviving evidence of the textile industry, which had been of some importance in the earlier part of the century. To provide lighting for the poorer parts of town, without the luxury

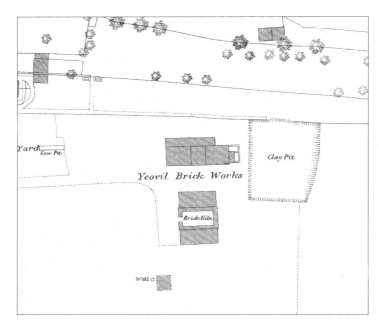

Yard Saw Pit

Yeovil Brick Works

Clay Pit

Brick Kiln

Well o

71 Left Yeovil Brick Works from the 1886 Ordnance Survey map, complete with brick kiln, clay pit and well

72 Opposite One of Yeovil's former coaching inns, the Three Choughs Hotel, on the corner of Hendford and South Street. February 2004. © B. and M. Gittos

of gas lighting, there was a candle factory on the north side of West Hendford between Salthouse Lane and Wellington Street. The town gas works, which had been opened in 1833 was on the corner of Middle Street and Station Road, adjacent to the Town Station. This was supplied by coal directly from the railway yard. In the gas works yard, there were three small turntables, only large enough for a single railway wagon, to enable the wagons to be switched between different lines in the constricted space of the yard. Next to the gas works, there were two wool stores, one fronting onto Middle Street. The other, in the rear adjoining the gas works, was owned by E.J. Farr and Company. This store had a private railway siding. Slightly further up Middle Street, on the northern side, there was a carriage works. There was also a coach factory between Park Road and Kingston which has long since disappeared, and now lies under the hospital roundabout. To provide a service for the more prosperous parts of the town, Yeovil Laundry was at the end of an alleyway in South Street, opposite the Greyhound public house. The cattle market site seems little changed in the area between North Lane and Court Ash. It is now mainly used as a car park, except on market days. In 1886 the lower third of the site was taken up by sheep pens. The auction yard on the other side of Court Ash also had sheep pens, but interestingly there seem to be no cattle pens shown. Next to the Cattle Market, beside North Lane, on what is now an empty plot opposite the entrance to North Lane car park stood one of the two slaughter houses identified on the map. The other, just off Vicarage Street, is now covered by part of the Marks and Spencer store.

The refreshment of the natives was assured by two breweries, one of which, Brutton's, was situated between Princes Street and Clarence Street, with a

malthouse opposite, on land which is now part of the Tesco car park. Brutton's premises were demolished in 2003 to make way for new housing. The other, the Royal Osborne Brewery was in Sherborne Road. This brewery had an aerated water works at the rear. There was also a Mineral and Aerated Water Works in Union Street, almost opposite the then police station. These refreshments were dispensed in the numerous public houses and hotels in the Yeovil of this period. Many survive, but some casualties can be mentioned. Perhaps the most notable was The George in Middle Street, demolished in 1962 (see Chapter 1). Another was the Castle Hotel, also in Middle Street, which was demolished in 1924. In the case of four of the establishments, evidence of their use as coaching inns can be seen, in the provision of a covered entrance into an inner yard. Two still exist, namely the Three Choughs *(72)* and The Mermaid, the other two being The George and the Castle, mentioned above. Whilst on the subject of horses there was a large yard with livery stables at the junction of Hendford and West Hendford. Another form of refreshment was provided by the Yeovil Dairy, which was situated in a yard at the northern end of Queen Street in an area now beneath the Queensway.

The spiritual needs of the population seem to have been well provided for with a wide selection of churches, chapels and Sunday schools. As well as St John's, there was Holy Trinity in Peter Street (marked on the map as having 'Seats for 600'). Holy Trinity had been built in the 1840s to alleviate the overcrowding then being experienced in St John's but has recently been converted into residential accommodation. In South Street, there was the Baptist chapel opposite the library, the façade of which has been incorporated into the new church, opened in 2003. Also in South Street there was a Methodist chapel

73 The façade (which is all that survives) of Yeovil's first National School, opened in 1846 and now incorporated into Tesco superstore. © B. and M. Gittos

near the southern end. The Vicarage Street Wesleyan Methodist chapel still stands, on the edge of the Quedam development. Christ Church, the Reformed Episcopalian church, was in Park Road, with a large Sunday School behind, in an area then known as Ram Park, part of which has become Sidney Gardens. The church and school were demolished in 1904 as a result of changing religious preferences. The Congregational chapel was set back from Princes Street, with its accompanying Sunday School behind on Clarence Street, which remains today.

The oldest school shown on the map is named as a Grammar School on Church Path. It was descended from the school which had been established in the old chantry chapel in 1573 (see Chapter 3). The first National School, which had opened in 1846, is shown in Huish. Part of this building was incorporated into the Tesco supermarket (73). The South Street School, opposite Union Street is also shown. This school was demolished in 1965. Kingston School stood between Kingston and Higher Kingston on a site now underneath the District Hospital. Yeovil's first Board School was in Reckleford, adjacent to Dampier Street, where it still stands opposite the Fire Station, although no longer a school.

By the time of the 1886 map, all four of Yeovil's railway stations were in existence but the first, at Hendford, had already closed for passenger traffic in 1861. Pen Mill Station had opened in 1856 and the Town Station in 1861. The foundation stone from the former Town Station, which is now in a flowerbed near the original site, gives the date 1860, as when building work commenced. A toll house, which had been built for the Yeovil and District Turnpike Trust in the 1760s is shown, although by this time long disused, at the foot of Hendford Hill. This disappeared with the building of the roundabout at the southern end of Queensway.

Of the public buildings shown, clearly the most important was the Town Hall and Market House in the High Street. Immediately behind are the Corn Exchange, Meat and Cheese Markets. This information from the 1886 map was extremely valuable in interpreting the archaeology of the Library Site (see Chapter 5). The fire station at this time was at the end of Vicarage Street, now under the corner of Marks and Spencer, and the police station was then in Union Street, in the Town House (now the home of Yeovil Town Council). The Municipal Swimming Pool is shown west of Felix Place, between Huish and West Hendford, close the entrance road to Tesco's car park. It was at this time a brand new facility, having opened in 1885. It was demolished just before the Tesco site was developed in 1992 and replaced by the Goldenstones Pool and Leisure Centre, off Brunswick Street. The hospital stood in the fork between Preston Road and Ilchester Road near to the present Fiveways round-about. The Union Workhouse was in Preston Road at Summerlands and on the corner of South Street and Bond Street, Woborn's Almshouse is shown. It was built in 1860 when it was moved from its original location behind the Pall Inn.

Ordnance Survey map, 1901
Perhaps one of the most interesting aspects of the Ordnance Survey's second edition of 1901 (scale 1:2,500) covering Yeovil is the fact that it provides a snapshot of the town just about a century ago. It brings home just how much has changed in that time. This map is based on the survey published in 1886 but with considerable updating. Seemingly, the only significant industrial development is the appearance of a dressing yard and brickworks, both on the corner of Kiddle's Lane and Sherborne Road. However, there is much to be seen with regard to the expansion of Yeovil's housing stock. New rows of terraced housing have appeared in Mill Lane and Kiddle's Lane and additional residential roads, have appeared in many locations. They can be found to the north, around Goldcroft, where King Street, Colmer Road and The Avenue have appeared, in the central area with Vincent Street and to the south, Belmont Street. Housing development is particularly noticeable to the east of the town in the region of Lyde Road. Camborne Street, Place and Grove have all appeared, together with Victoria Road. In the same area, Cromwell Road is partially built up, whilst Alexandra Road and St Michael's Road are in the course of construction. There has been some activity to the west, between West Hendford and Hendford where Manor Road and Everton Road are apparently being built, with Orchard Street and Beer Street linking Huish to West Hendford.

What is very clear from the 1901 map is that most of the housing development sites are occupying single fields (74). By referring back to the

1842 Tithe map the field names can be identified. Cromwell Road was built on 'Priddles Mead' and Victoria Road (75) on 'West Beachams Close'. The western part of St Michael's Road, only shown in outline, together with the church of St Michael and All Angels, lie within the bounds of 'Goar Knap'. Alexandra Road was another example which at its northern end joined a lane, then known as Sydling Lane, later to become the western part of Roseberry Avenue. It was situated wholly within 'Little Hather Mead' and on its western side the present back garden boundaries are coincident with the edge of the field. Only a few houses are shown in Cromwell Road, the former 'Priddles Mead'. This phenomenon was not restricted to the east of the town because, just to the north, an L-shaped plot known as 'Pound Close', between Higher Kingston and Goldcroft, was used for the development comprising Colmer Road and The Avenue. All this growth meant that Yeovil had burst its boundaries, with Alexandra Road, Victoria Road and the Camborne estate all lying outside the borough. To meet the spiritual needs of the growing population in the east of the town, a new parish of St Michael's was established in 1897 (76). St Michael's church was built beside the road which would later adopt its name but in 1901 was still known as Brickyard Lane. The map shows the new church initially standing in open country, very different from its situation today.

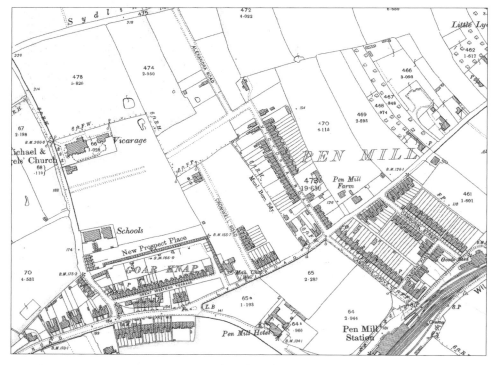

74 The Pen Mill area from the 1901 Ordnance Survey map, showing new housing occupying the former fields

75 Above Victoria Road, Yeovil, occupying a field identifiable as West Beachams Close from the 1842 Tithe map. © *B. and M. Gittos*

76 Right Detail from the entrance to the church of St Michael and All Angels, which was built on a field called Goar Knap. © *B. and M. Gittos*

Ordnance Survey map, 1938

The 1938 Ordnance Survey (scale 1:10,560 or 6in to 1 mile) map demonstrates the rapid pace of development of Yeovil up to the Second World War. For the first time, orchards are no longer a distinctive feature of the area. Two aspects are very noticeable: firstly, the extent of development since 1901 and, secondly, the many further programmes underway at the time. Of the new features shown, the most prominent by far is the appearance, for the first time, of the Westland factory and airfield. At the other end of town a sewage works is shown south-east of Pen Mill Station, just across the railway line. This, Yeovil's first sewage treatment works, had opened in 1903. Up until that time the town had relied on more primitive methods. The isolation hospital is still shown amongst areas of allotments, where the Lyde Road Trading Estate is now situated. This had been enlarged by the Yeovil Corporation in 1893 and in 1903. On the corner of Sherborne Road and Newton Road there is a large building, the premises of Aplin & Barrett, the dairy products firm which had moved to the site. Just west of the town centre, the football ground at Huish is now shown. Horsey Lane seems to have changed again, to an L-shaped route from the Hendford Stone Works beside the railway line just east of the Westland factory, to the junction with Beer Street and West Hendford. Here it turns right, heading to meet the junction of Hendford and Hendford Hill.

As far as new housing developments are concerned, to the west of the town there is the small estate for Westland employees, comprising Westland Road and Seaton Road on what was originally the main approach to the factory. Nearby, a previously undeveloped length of Beer Street is now established as West Street. North of the town centre there is growth in the guise of Mitchelmore Road, named after Alderman William Mitchelmore. Housing in Goldcroft now extends north to Sparrow Road, while King Street has additional properties. Crofton Park has filled in the open space south of Colmer Road. In the east Southville, Eastville and Westville have been created, with a school just to the south west, replacing the dressing yard and brickworks shown on the 1901 map. Sydling Lane has been extended to meet Lyde Road and renamed Rosebery Avenue. Building along St Michael's Road and Cromwell Road has been completed and Alexandra Road has housing on its western side, with a glove factory and dressing yard to the east.

Of the areas shown as under development or laid out, the vast majority are to the north. The new location for Yeovil School, between Goldcroft and Mudford Road, is shown as under construction. Lower Larkhill Lane is being developed and has now been renamed Stiby Road, to the north of which, Marl Close and Coronation Avenue are building, the latter in celebration of the new king. Marl Close is located entirely within a single field, demonstrating that the process of building streets of houses field by field was still happening. Marl Close Farm, to the east of Coronation Avenue, survives within a built-up area. To the south of Stiby Road, the Westfield estate is growing and, leading off Preston Road, two cul-de-sacs, Cedar Grove and Home Drive now occupy two former fields. There is more development south of Preston Road. Glenthorne Avenue, then a cul-de-sac off Mudford Road, can be seen to be following a field boundary. In the east, Highfield Road has been constructed from Gordon Road, following the line of an existing footpath to meet St Michael's Avenue. South of the town there is some infilling along West Coker Road, together with new residences on Sandhurst Road, Wraxhill Road and Beaconsfield Road.

Snell map, 1950

Although the 1950 Snell map is only a basic town street map, it can still provide information about the early post-war period. No buildings are shown, but the up to date street pattern is useful. Some new streets are shown, the most extensive being in the region of Larkhill. This was due to the construction of 150 prefabricated houses in this area in 1946. Stiby Road, the former Lower Larkhill Lane, is still a cul-de-sac ending at Marl Close, with open country between there and Larkhill Road. In the north-east, Glenthorne Avenue has been extended as far as St Michael's Avenue and Chelston, St George's and Elmhurst Avenues have been created.

Ordnance Survey map, 1958

The first post-war Ordnance Survey map, published in 1958, shows clear evidence of expansion. Again, this is occurring mainly to the north of the town, such as in Stiby Road, which has been extended to meet Larkhill Road. To meet the needs of this area, there are now two schools for infants and primary children west of Westfield Road. Alongside Larkhill Road the Yeovil greyhound racetrack is still present. Two major new schools have been built in the north-east, Bucklers Mead and Grass Royal Junior. A significant aspect of the 1958 map is that it shows the town just prior to the major changes involved with the building of the District Hospital, the sweeping away of the old Town Station and the putting through of the Queensway.

Ordnance Survey map, 1988

The Ordnance Survey map published in 1988 (1:25,000), but corrected only to 1985, shows Yeovil much enlarged, with both additional housing and industrial estates, reflecting a broad-based and growing economy. In the local government reorganisation of 1974, Yeovil had lost its borough status and been subsumed into Yeovil District Council (since renamed South Somerset District Council). However, the existing town boundaries remained in place.

In the north-western part of town the Larkhill prefab estate has been replaced by the permanent housing of Abbey Road and Monks Dale while Marl Close Farm has disappeared under Thatcham Park. Westfield Secondary School has been built to cater for a growing population. The greyhound racetrack has gone although the site has not yet been reused and the Larkhill Soling factory has been constructed. Major expansion is clear around the former Houndstone and Lufton Camps. The changes which have occurred since 1958 are very striking to the north-east of the town with major new housing between Mudford Road and Lyde Road. This includes a new school, Birchfield Primary. Lyde Road has grown the Pen Mill Industrial Estate; Pittards leather factory now occupies its present position and there is a new sewage works close to the River Yeo.

The local landscape has also been changed by the closure of the Yeovil to Taunton railway line in 1964 and the subsequent construction of Lysander Road. Work has begun on the Lynx Trading Estate much of which lies outside the town boundary. South of Lysander Road, extensive new housing is centred on Plantagenet Chase and Forest Hill. Further development at Westland has seen the disappearance of the Cricket Ground and the allotment gardens south of Westland Road.

Ordnance Survey map, 1994

Because of the short period which had elapsed since the 1988 map, the changes seen on the 1994 map (1:25,000) are relatively minor. The only significant development has taken place on the Abbey Manor estate, straddling the town boundary. It spreads northwards but there is still a distinct gap to the east before Monks Dale is reached. The new facilities include a primary school to replace Preston Primary, a community centre, medical centre and a supermarket. Outside the town boundary, the site of the former army camps, at Houndstone and Lufton have now become a business park and trading estate respectively. To the south-west, new housing is surrounding Sampson's Wood, a process moving towards completion with the building of Watercombe Heights. In the sporting arena, Yeovil's famous sloping football pitch at Huish has given way to a Tesco superstore. The new football ground, nostalgically named Huish Park, is shown in its current out of town location, on the edge of the old Lufton Camp. The Yeovil Ski Centre, on the lower slopes of Summerhouse Hill, is also identified.

SUMMARY

Although not a comprehensive survey of the maps of Yeovil, from the selection reviewed, it has been possible to discover the contribution which maps can make to studying the archaeology of any area. Their value in amplifying and augmenting the historical record has been well demonstrated. From the nineteenth-century material, the Tithe map and the 1886 OS map stand out, the former with its social history of land ownership and tenancy and the latter with the fine detail resulting from a survey at 1:500. The twentieth-century maps show much information which could be laboriously teased out from written sources but which maps conveniently present as a series of snapshots. One important picture which has emerged from this study concerns the piecemeal development of Yeovil over a long period, field by field. Whilst it is fascinating to relate the former field names to individual blocks of housing, this process has also provided a remarkable legacy. Effectively, much of the field pattern which surrounded the town in the nineteenth century has become fossilised within the layout of roads and houses which make up the modern town. The twenty-first century townscape is, in part, a replica of the former rural landscape and some of Yeovil's medieval past lives on in today's concrete, bricks and mortar.

CHAPTER 7

SURVIVING EVIDENCE OF WARTIME YEOVIL

Jack Sweet

The twentieth century was a century of conflict, and there were few years when a war was not being fought somewhere in the world. However, the First and Second World Wars were the most destructive, resulting in the deaths of tens of millions of people and the laying to waste of whole countries. In common with most communities in the United Kingdom, Yeovil did not escape the effects of these two major conflicts, some evidence of which remains, and can still be seen at the time of writing, in the autumn of 2003.

THE FIRST WORLD WAR

The war which broke out in August 1914, and which was confidently expected to be over by Christmas, was primarily fought on the European continent and, when the Armistice brought the conflict to an end four years later, in November 1918, millions had died in the titanic struggle. Physically, the war did not touch Yeovil, but with many hundreds of its men and women serving in the fighting forces on land, sea and in the air, its effects were felt by nearly every family in the town. Over 220 young men of Yeovil died in the conflict, and several hundred more suffered wounds or disease. The names of the fallen are inscribed on two war memorials, one in the Borough and a second on Preston Road. Two buildings still exist in the town which evoke the era of the First World War. One of these was used during the conflict as a military hospital and the other, comprising a pair of houses, is to a design inspired by an army hut.

77 The Newnam Memorial Hall, home to the Red Cross Military Hospital from 1915 to 1919.
Photo Jack W. Sweet

The Red Cross Hospital in South Street

The horrendously high casualties being suffered on the Western Front by the British Army placed a tremendous strain on the nation's military and civilian hospitals and across the country, public halls, large houses and many other buildings were adapted to treat the thousands of wounded. In 1915, the Trustees of the Baptist Schools granted the British Red Cross Society the free use of the Newnam Memorial Hall on South Street (now part of Pegasus Court), for a 62 bed auxiliary military hospital, and by the time the last wounded soldier left in 1919, over 1200 men had been nursed back to health *(77)*. The wounded were brought to the hall straight from the hospital ships to be nursed by a small trained staff assisted by volunteers from the Somerset/80 (Women) and Somerset/19 (Men) Voluntary Aid Detachments (VAD). Although many of the wounded were very ill when they arrived, only four died from the 1200 treated, which reflected great credit on the skill and dedication of the medical and nursing staff. The hospital was never short of support from the people of Yeovil who provided funds, hospitality and entertainment for the men. At a gathering of the organisations who had helped with the running of the hospital, the County Director of the British Red Cross Society said that he believed the presence of the 'boys in blue', (wounded servicemen wore light blue jackets and trousers) had made the people of Yeovil much better citizens. There is a plaque on the wall of the building which commemorates its use as a Red Cross hospital and which reads:

This Stone
is erected by the
Yeovil Town Council
in grateful recognition
of the splendid services
rendered on behalf of the town by the
British Red Cross Society
in providing a hospital for the care of
1200 sailors & soldiers and to the Baptist Church
for the generous loan of
these premises for the purpose
during the Great War 1915–1919
Alderman W.R.E. Mitchelmore,
Mayor of Yeovil

The Nissen-Petren houses (78)

During the First World War, tens of thousands of corrugated iron huts with semicircular roofs, based on the designs of Lieutenant Colonel P.N. Nissen DSO, Royal Engineers, were built to meet the demands of the armed forces. The Nissen Bow Hut could be constructed almost anywhere, quickly and efficiently. In the years immediately following the end of hostilities, housing was one the most serious problems facing the nation. Sources of materials, labour and cash were stretched and local authorities were wrestling with shortages, the lack of houses and the skilled labour to build them. The Yeovil Borough Council had been one of the pioneering housing authorities in the years before the war, and was anxious to continue to provide houses to meet the acute need in the town. In March 1922 the Chairman of the Housing Committee stated:

> There are more than 600 applicants for houses in the Borough at the present time, and over 400 of these applicants are lodging with their families in very overcrowded conditions. This in itself is considered sufficient for the urgency of the situation.

Again in 1923, the Chairman is recorded as saying that the council:

> Must provide houses, we have a limited time in which to do it. The people expect and entreat us to provide houses of some sort or another.

The scene was set for the Borough Council to look for quickly built and inexpensive houses to meet the need.

In November 1924, it appeared that the answer had been found. At that month's meeting, the council took what they thought would be an important

78 The Nissen-Petren prototype houses in Goldcroft. *Photo Jack W. Sweet*

step towards solving the town's housing crisis. A local firm of architects, Messrs Petter and Warren, presented plans showing a pair of experimental 'Nissen-Petren' houses of a unique design and method of construction. It was estimated that they could be built for £350 or possibly less per house. The houses used a new type of roof construction based on Lieutenant Colonel Nissen's design. This was unique in that the main framework of the roof consisted of semicircular steel ribs, both ends of which were bolted to the concrete foundations of the building supporting the whole weight of the roof. It was entirely independent of the walls, and there would be considerable saving in the cost of building load bearing exterior walls estimated to be about £100 per house. The roof would be put on at an early stage and included a patent metal covering with an inner sheet of steel, suitably waterproofed. It was claimed by Messrs Petter and Warren that the early roofing of the building would enable the interior walls, chimney breasts and fireplaces to be built irrespective of the weather. The houses would be built of concrete and mass produced from factory-made components. Therefore, most of the construction work could be carried out very quickly, by unskilled labour. The Nissen-Petren house would have a scullery, bathroom, w.c., larder, living room and one bedroom on the ground floor with two bedrooms upstairs. To the Borough Council, the houses appeared to be the answer to their problems. They would be cheap, quickly built and provide good accommodation. Work began on two prototype houses in Goldcroft at the end of 1924. The architects were so certain that the design would be popular, that they formed a company entitled The Nissen-Petren

Houses Ltd with the object of providing local authorities with plans of the houses and the organisation and supervision of the manufacture of the standardised components. The directors of the company included Sir Ernest Petter of Westland Aircraft and oil engine fame, and Lieutenant Colonel Nissen.

Some four months later in March 1925, the pair of Nissen-Petren houses was finished, and the council carried out an official inspection, followed by visits from representatives of the War Office, Air Ministry, public authorities and the London press. A great demand was foreseen for Nissen-Petren houses. In September 1925, the final accounts were presented and the cost was £1027 3s 3d making the cost of each house £513 11s 7d – some £160 more than the estimate. The architects, however, considered this increase was justified by the experimental nature of the project. The economies of standardisation were not available and, proportionately, more men had been employed than would be required for a large scheme. They believed that large-scale development would reduce the cost, and the Housing Committee chairman told the council that the War Office and the Admiralty had decided to build houses of this design for married quarters, and houses with slight alterations were being built throughout the country. However, one member of the council hoped that the authority would embark on no more such costly experiments. The Borough Council, it seems, adopted this advice, because no more Nissen-Petren houses were built in Yeovil. The Yeovil Rural District Council, however, had a little more faith in the design than the borough, because they built some Nissen-Petren houses at Barwick, South Petherton and West Camel.

How many Nissen-Petren houses were built is not known but the pair in Goldcroft was the first. They are unique, being the prototype of a house which the designers and patrons believed would herald a leap forward in providing houses cheaply and quickly for the thousands of families who needed them. In 1983, the Department of the Environment listed the Goldcroft houses as being of Special Architectural Interest. Few, if any, of the tens of thousands of Nissen huts built during the First World War survive 90 years later, but the Goldcroft Nissen-Petren houses remain as a peaceful legacy of that conflict.

THE SECOND WORLD WAR

On 1 September 1939, only 21 years from the Armistice of 11 November 1918 which had brought the First World War to an end, Nazi Germany invaded Poland, and the war which followed was fought on a global scale. The surrender of the Japanese in August 1945 ended the Second World War, which had directly or indirectly involved most of the world's nations. Unlike the First World War, which had principally involved the military of the opposing powers, the Second was total war, in which civilian populations were subjected to the horrors of war on land, sea and from the air. In Yeovil the war affected everything. There were air raids, civilians and military personnel were killed and wounded, property was destroyed and damaged while nights were spent in air-raid shelters listening to the drone of German aircraft overhead and wondering whose turn it was to be bombed. During 1939/40 many hundreds of people were evacuated to the town from the London area, to avoid the heavy bombing of the capital. There was the blackout, rationing of food and clothes, little travel for pleasure or holidays and there were large camps built at Houndstone and Lufton for the army (now the sites of business parks, residential estates and the Huish Park Football Stadium). At Yeovilton a new station was built for the Fleet Air Arm. From 1942 onwards there were the Americans preparing for the D-Day invasion, with hospitals at Houndstone and Lufton to care for their wounded returning from the campaign in north-west Europe. Yeovilians served and fought in all the theatres of war on land, sea and in the air and, sadly, 60 died. Although nearly 60 years have passed since the end of the Second World War and Yeovil has changed greatly, there remains a rapidly diminishing number of reminders of the six years of conflict. Some of these are described here and the author apologises for any omissions or inaccuracies in the telling.

Pillboxes

The German offensive in the West, the evacuation of the British Army from Dunkirk, and the fall of France in June 1940, brought the enemy to the French coast and the real threat of invasion of our country. During the summer of 1940, defences against invasion were built across England, incorporating thousands of pillboxes and strongpoints. The pillbox was generally designed for all round defence, loopholed for machine-guns or rifles, with walls and roof covering thick enough to be bullet and splinter-proof. Some were built with sufficient strength to be shell-proof and larger pillboxes housed anti-tank guns.

In the event of invasion, it was planned that Yeovil would form an anti-tank island, defended by the Yeovil Borough Company of the 3rd (Yeovil) Battalion Somerset Home Guard, supported by the 208th LAA Training Regiment, Royal Artillery from Houndstone Camp. The anti-tank island comprised a pillbox strongpoint on Summerhouse Hill, covering approaches from the south in the direction of Barwick and an outer and inner circle of road blocks, designed to hold up and delay the passage of enemy tanks and other vehicles approaching from the south or west. The outer road blocks would be placed at the top of Hendford Hill, supported by a pillbox strongpoint in the front garden of No.166 and at Newton Road railway bridge. The inner road blocks, at which anti-tank obstacles of triangular iron rails and concrete tubes would be placed, were to be sited at Huish near the junction with West Street; West Street; Westland Road near the junction with Beer Street; Beer Street near the junction with West Hendford; West Hendford near the junction with Beer Street; Hendford near the junction with Brunswick Street; Brunswick Street

79 Above The pillbox strongpoint on Summerhouse Hill. *Photo Jack W. Sweet*

80 Right The pillbox at the top of Hendford Hill. *Photo Jack W. Sweet*

near the junction with Penn Hill; Addlewell Lane, northern and southern ends; Stars Lane near the junction with Summerhouse Terrace; Station Road near the junction with Middle Street and Newton Road near the junction with Sherborne Road. Company Headquarters would be at the Municipal Offices in King George Street with the reserve and quartermaster's stores at the Southville Drill Hall.

Thankfully the invasion never came, and the Yeovil anti-tank island was never put to the test. However, the Summerhouse Hill pillbox still stands looking south to the feared invasion route *(79)*, and the pillbox on Hendford Hill still commands this main road into town *(80)*.

The Balloon Barrage and Anti-aircraft Defences

The Royal Air Force Balloon Barrages were a form of static defence designed to force enemy aircraft to fly higher and therefore bomb less accurately or to deter dive-bombing attacks. The LZ (Low Zone) Balloon, the main component of the barrages, was approximately 62ft long (19m) and 25ft (7.6m)

131

in diameter and filled with hydrogen gas. With three air-filled stabilising fins, the balloon was designed to fly at an altitude of 5000ft (1524m) attached by a steel cable to a mobile winch. The balloon barrages were controlled by Balloon Command, divided into Groups and Balloon Barrage Squadrons. Initially the balloon barrage was formed to defend London but was soon extended to major provincial cities, and on 31 May 1940, the Air Ministry instructed the barrage to cover factories engaged in the vital task of aircraft production, including the Westland Works at Yeovil. On 24 July 1940, No.957 (Balloon) Squadron arrived in Yeovil with 24 balloons. Squadron Headquarters was established in Braggchurch, Hendford Hill, and during the next four years the barrage balloon sites set up in and around the town included: Aldon; Barwick Park; Bunford; Coronation Avenue; East Coker Road/Sandhurst Road; Grass Royal; Higher Kingston Recreation Ground; Larkhill Lane; Lufton Camp; Marl Close; Preston Grove; West Hendford; Westland Works and Yew Tree Close.

The barrage was raised when enemy aircraft were reported to be approaching Yeovil and even without hostile activity, the flying of the barrage was not without incident. Balloons were vulnerable to lightning strikes and high winds. There was also the danger of machine-gun attack by enemy aircraft. In March and April of 1941 alone, five balloons were destroyed by lightning and one broke adrift in a high wind to come down in East Chinnock. On 7 October 1940, following the first heavy air raid on Yeovil, there was an unexploded bomb by the Larkhill Lane site. The crew of the balloon at Yew Tree Close had a lucky escape on the night of 8 May 1941, when a German bomber struck the cable and dropped its bombs on the site. Fortunately there were no casualties but the crew's accommodation hut was smashed. There were reports of the balloon barrage being machine-gunned on 9 August 1942. Repairs to the balloons were carried out in St Michael's Hall as this was the only building in the town with sufficient internal length and height to enable the balloon to be inflated to check the repair. In June 1944, the Germans unleashed their V1 flying bombs on London and the Home Counties, and on 21 June No.957 (Balloon) Squadron was sent from Yeovil to the south coast to join the Anti-Diver measures set up to combat this menace. As a reminder of all this activity, the mooring blocks of the Aldon barrage balloon site survive (81).

During 1940, anti-aircraft (AA) guns were brought and located around the area to defend the Westland Works. Four heavy 3.7in (94mm) AA guns were installed on the Showground by the Dorchester Road, and Bofors Light AA guns were placed on various sites, including one at the top of Hendford Hill near the Quicksilver Mail public house, and another next to the bridge over the former railway line by Bunford Lane on the south side of the airfield. Positions were also set up for machine guns. The guns were manned by regular soldiers and members of the local Home Guard. Owing to the temporary nature of the gun positions no evidence remains. Searchlights also formed part

81 Mooring blocks of the Aldon barrage balloon. *Photo Jack W. Sweet*

of anti-aircraft defence and, with their strong beams of light, sought to pick out enemy aircraft at night for the anti-aircraft guns to attempt to shoot down. The searchlight batteries were mobile and placed near potential targets such as the Westland Works. No evidence remains of the searchlight batteries set up around Yeovil, but a Somerset Civil Defence report of 7 May 1941 tells of an enemy plane over Yeovil firing down a searchlight beam and then being seen to crash in flames to the east.

An important element in the nation's anti-aircraft defences was the Royal Observer Corps (the title Royal was granted in 1941) which provided a nation-wide, round-the-clock system of spotting and identifying enemy aircraft crossing the country and was essential for the efficient operation of the air raid warning system. The Corps, which was primarily staffed by volunteers, identified, tracked and reported the passage of all aircraft, friend or foe, from observer posts on high hills or other prominent positions, in clusters of two to four posts, linked to group centres. The information was passed to Fighter Group and Sector Operations Rooms and up to Fighter Command. No.22 Group Centre was located at the top of the Southwoods cul-de-sac, off Hendford Hill. The Royal Observer Corps was stood down on 12 May 1945, four days after VE-Day, but with the threat from the Soviet Union and nuclear war, the Corps was reactivated in 1947, and from 1957 to 1991 the Corps was given the important role of measuring and reporting on the onset, location and after-effects of a possible nuclear attack. However, with the collapse of the Soviet Union and the advance of technology to detect nuclear explosions and fallout, the Corps was again stood down in 1991.

The Southwoods Group Headquarters was completely rebuilt in 1963 and closed some years ago. The site has now been sold.

During the Second World War many forms of camouflage were used extensively to break up the outlines of buildings or disguise their use from the prying eyes of enemy aircraft. One method was to paint factories or commercial premises to resemble domestic property. Several large factory buildings at Westland were camouflaged to resemble houses and the aerodrome marked out to represent a number of fields. On the south side of the Top Ten Bingo Club, Stars Lane (the old Gaumont cinema), the faded paint work of the attempt to camouflage this large wall as two detached houses can still be seen from the adjoining car park *(colour plate 4)*.

Air-raid shelters

With the fall of France in June 1940, the whole of the south and west of England was well within the range of German bombers, and attacks began on Somerset with bombs on Flax Bourton, near Bristol, on 18 June. Yeovil had already put in hand plans to provide air-raid shelters, and on 4 July 1940, the Borough Council announced in the *Western Gazette* that shelters were available for 1195 people in specially adapted cellars in business and private premises. The council stated, however, that the shelters were for people who might be caught in the streets during an air raid, and not for the protection of nearby residents. The shelters were provided in the following premises: No.19 High Street; Western Counties Stores, Church Street entrance; Redwoods, The Borough; Harbour and Hobbs, Vicarage Street; Confectionery Dept, Co-operative Society, Middle Street; Bakery Dept, Co-operative Society, Vicarage Street; Dunn & Co, Middle Street (rear entrance Vicarage Street); Brutton's Cellars, Clarence Street; British Legion, Princes Street; Dr Unwin, Kingston House, Kingston; Mr T. Moore's Stables, Higher Kingston; Holman & Ney's, Hendford; Dupont, No.63 Hendford and Brooks, Dentist, Hendford. They were also under construction at: Radio House, Princes Street at the entrance to Quik Auto Motor Body Works, Park Road; No.13 Kingston adjoining Duke of York Inn and Mr Buchanan's House, North Lane. In giving these details in its July edition, the *Yeovil Review* advised housewives and others likely to be in the town during the day, to cut out the article and carry it with them so that they would be acquainted with the exact location of the shelter, should the occasion arise.

At the meeting of the Borough Council on 9 September, the Mayor stated his concern at:

> The behaviour of certain irresponsible people in the air raid shelters... was absolutely disgusting and decent people refused to use the shelters. It was only a small percentage of people who made themselves a complete nuisance to others and he hoped they would remain outside and expose themselves to whatever dangers existed.

On 9 November 1940 it was reported that shelters had been provided for 2900 people and accommodation for another 500 was under construction. By 10 February 1941, the Borough Council announced that the total number of domestic, communal and other forms of shelter could now accommodate 3075, with work in hand for another 1704. However the misuse of public shelters continued and it was reported that three had to be thoroughly scrubbed out and cleansed before they could be used.

A report to the Borough Council's Invasion Committee on 30 September 1942 on the provision of air-raid shelters in Yeovil stated that the total number of persons who could be accommodated had reached 16233 as follows:

		TYPE	ACCOMMODATION PERSONS
(i)	Public:	Trenches	40
		Surface	640
		Basement	1,675
		Schools etc	1,444
(ii)	Surface Communal Domestic		8,165
(iii)	Basement Communal Domestic		144
(iv)	Anderson		528
(v)	Morrison		3,045
(vi)	Privately-owned constructed shelters		552
		TOTAL	16,233

The Surface Communal Domestic shelter was generally constructed of brick or concrete block and was designed to withstand all but the direct hit from a bomb. The shelters were usually erected in the back gardens of houses and shared by several householders and their families. Anderson Shelters were issued free, early in the war, to householders and comprised a number of curved sheets of corrugated iron assembled to form an arch with wooden ends, one being used as the entrance. The shelter was sunk into the ground, usually in the back garden, and covered with a protective layer of earth. The Morrison shelter was for use indoors and named after Mr Herbert Morrison, the Home Secretary in 1941, when the shelters were issued free to householders. The shelter, which was assembled by the householder, was composed of four welded mesh sides and a base with a strong solid metal top. As with most surface air-raid shelters, the Morrison could not protect its occupants from a direct bomb hit but provided substantial protection from falling masonry in the event of a near miss.

On 11 September 1944, following the advance of the Allied armies across France and into Belgium, the threat of air attack on Yeovil had become virtually non-existent, and the Borough Council decided to close all public air-raid shelters. In 1947, the Communal Domestic air-raid shelters were sold to the householder on whose land each stood for the sum of £1 1s 0d, and many of the

82 Surface communal domestic air-raid shelters at the rear of Goldcroft. *Photo Jack W. Sweet*

83 Left One of the air-raid shelters provided for the children of Pen Mill Primary School. *Photo Jack W. Sweet*

84 Below A privately constructed underground air-raid shelter in Mudford Road. *Photo Jack W. Sweet*

brick or concrete structures can still be found serving a variety of domestic purposes *(82, 83, 84)*. A fading yellow capital letter S followed by the even more faded 13 persons can just be read on the wall of the Yeovil Centre facing Reckleford, and indicates the entrance to a former public communal air-raid shelter.

The Air Raids

Yeovil air-raid warning sirens were placed on the roof of the police station, now the Magistrates' Court on Petters Way, on Yeovil School, Mudford Road, and on the roof of No.166 Hendford Hill, and warnings were sounded on 365 occasions from Friday 5 July 1940 to Friday 16 June 1944. People took to the air-raid shelters listening for the sound of approaching enemy aircraft and wondering whether this time, bombs would fall on the town. On 355 occasions the enemy passed over heading for other targets such as Bristol, the cities and ports of South Wales or the north west of England. Quite often the raiders did not come: it might be a false alarm or the enemy changed direction. The length of time between the warning and the 'all clear' being sounded, could last for hours or a few minutes. During the night of 16 January 1941 the warning lasted for nearly 11 hours whereas it was only five minutes on the following 22 March.

However, on ten occasions, with the Westland Aircraft Works as the obvious target, bombs fell on Yeovil. On Monday 30 September 1940, a force of German bombers set out to attack the Westland Works, but heavy clouds covered the target, and bombing blind, the aircraft released their bombs over Sherborne causing considerable damage and killing 18 and injuring 30 townspeople.

Raid one: Monday 7 October 1940

On Monday 7 October, the German bombers came again and this time Yeovil was attacked by a force of 20 Junkers Ju 88s. The warning was sounded at 3.45pm and some ten minutes later 33 high-explosive bombs and 18 oil fire bombs fell on the town killing 16 people and wounding another 29. Bombs fell on Montague Burton's shop next to Woolworths in Middle Street; the Vicarage Street Methodist Church; Rickett's glove factory at Addlewell Lane; on Roping Road; Summerleaze Park and St Andrew's Road. There were unexploded bombs in Park Street, at the junction of Preston Road and St Andrew's Road and next to the barrage balloon site by Larkhill Lane. Some of the oil bombs did not ignite, including one in Mitchelmore Road and another in Everton Road. Several houses in St Andrew's Road near the junction with Preston Road still bear shrapnel marks from the exploding bombs which fell in the area, and the main front door of Parcroft School (formerly Summerleaze Park School) has shrapnel scars from the bomb which exploded in Summerleaze Park. A number of bombs also left craters in the school playing field. No bombs fell on the target, Westland Works.

The following 16 people lost their lives in the first raid:

Air-raid shelter at Vicarage Street Methodist Church: Mrs F. Lumber;
  Mrs W. Bright; Mrs V. Pickard and Mrs M. Bugler

Montague Burton's shop: Mr R. Batstone; Mrs F. Batstone; Mr F.
  Palmer; Mr F. Rose; Mr N. Gay; Mr W. Tucker; Mrs E. Smith and Mrs
  L. Johnson

Summerleaze Park: Mr C. Rendell

No.25 St Andrew's Road: Mrs A. Hayward

Air-raid shelter at No.45 Grove Avenue: Mr L. Forsey and Mrs M.
  Morris

Raid two: Tuesday 8 October 1940

Between 7.20pm and 7.30pm, a small force of enemy aircraft scattered 44 high-explosive bombs over the western part of Yeovil, with Preston Grove and Westbourne Grove bearing the brunt. The raid left 11 people dead from a direct hit on a private air-raid shelter in the garden of No.103 Preston Grove, and three people in the vicinity were injured. Five houses were destroyed and 50 damaged. The 11 people who lost their lives were: Mrs M. Heywood; Mrs M. Harrison; Mr W. Fitkin; Mrs O. Fitkin; Maxwell Fitkin (three years); Laurence Sweet (nine years); Miss J. Dodge; Miss J. Young and there were also three unidentified bodies, including one female and one child.

Raid three: Saturday 12 October 1940

The warning was sounded at 8.15pm and a lone German bomber dropped five high-explosive bombs on the town centre. One person was seriously injured and four slightly. Church House on Church Street was badly damaged, and some stained glass windows in the south wall of St John's Church were smashed by blast and debris. Other bombs fell in Park Street and at the back of a house on Penn Hill, partly demolishing the building and damaging the adjoining South Street Infants School (Belmont House now stands on the site of the school). On 12 and 14 October, Houndstone Camp was bombed and 18 soldiers were killed in the two attacks with another 48 wounded.

Raid four: Wednesday 16 October 1940

During the evening bombs fell on Mudford Road destroying five houses and damaging another 17. Three occupants of No.122 Mudford Road were injured.

Raid five: Wednesday 26 March 1941

The air-raid warning sounded at 11am and just before 12 noon, a single Dornier Do17 bomber dived across the town from the east aiming at the Westland Works and dropped six high-explosive bombs in a line towards the factory. Four bombs fell on the adjoining Westland housing estate and two on the factory. The official summary of the raid reported that of the two bombs which fell on the factory, one 250kg bomb penetrated the roof of the sub-assembly shop at an angle, struck the ground 180ft (55m) from where it entered, ricocheted and travelled for 240ft (73m), exploding opposite the office building where nearly all the windows front and back were broken by blast. Walls were heavily marked by splinters. In the erecting shop, a large number of holes made by splinters resulted in work being held up for a night. The second and smaller bomb of 50kg exploded in the flying ground leaving a crater 4ft by 6ft (1.2m x 1.8m). The bombs on the nearby houses in Westland Terrace (now Road) destroyed or damaged beyond repair 11 houses and damaged a further 132. Three men, five women and a five year old boy were killed, four of the dead were Westland employees, and 36 injured. The names of those who died were:

In Westland Works: Mrs H. Mulhall; Mrs A. Hann; Mr J. Palmer and
   Mr L. Pritchard
In Westland Terrace: Miss M. Guy; Mrs L. Hoyle; Trevor Hoyle (five
   years); Mrs J. Culvert and Mr E. Neville

Raid six: Good Friday 11 April 1941
Between the warning at 9.40pm on Good Friday evening and 3.40am the following morning, several delayed action bombs were dropped on the town centre. These bombs were designed to cause the maximum disruption (because no one knew if or when they would explode) and to cause maximum casualties to the emergency services dealing with them. All the bombs exploded before the 'all clear' was sounded, destroying the Corn Exchange behind the King George Street Municipal Offices (now occupied by the Halifax Bank), Boots the Chemist by the Borough (the site of Burger King) and neighbouring shops, as well as seriously damaging other nearby property. Soldiers of The King's Own Scottish Borderers were billeted in the Corn Exchange, and four were killed and five injured. Patrol Officer Charles Gillard of the Auxiliary Fire Service was killed when the delayed action bomb exploded as he fought the fire in the Corn Exchange and another fireman was seriously injured; ten civilians were also injured in the raid. A memorial to Patrol Officer Gillard can

85 The memorial to Patrol Officer Charles Gillard placed on the remains of the wall of the old Corn Exchange, in the Borough Arcade, near the spot where he was killed in the bombing on Good Friday 1941. *Photo Jack W. Sweet*

be seen on the remains of the Corn Exchange wall adjoining the Borough Arcade between High Street and South Street *(85)*.

Raid seven: Thursday 8 May 1941
At midnight a German bomber struck the steel cable of the barrage balloon at the Yew Tree Close site and dropped its bombs. There were no casualties but the balloon crew's living accommodation was smashed. The remaining bombs fell harmlessly in adjoining fields.

Raid eight: Friday 16 May 1941
A single enemy aircraft dropped seven high-explosive bombs in fields from Stone Lane to Mudford Road near the junction with St Michael's Avenue, at around midnight. The explosions caused minor damage to windows and doors in the vicinity; there were no human casualties, but a cow was killed and another injured.

Raid nine: Sunday 25 May 1941
At two minutes past midnight on Sunday morning, after flying low over the town three times with its navigation lights on, a single German aircraft dropped 14 high-explosive bombs on Mudford Road. Five people, including a boy, were killed, seven injured, eight houses destroyed and 115 damaged. For many years after the war shrapnel damage could be seen on the Mudford Road water tower. Slight difference in the colour of roof tiles of some houses in the vicinity bears witness to the repairs carried out following the raid. The people who died were: Mr D. Haines; Mrs R. Haines; Miss K. Denmead; Mrs A. Bell and Dennis Gillingham (nine years).

Raid ten: Wednesday 5 August 1942
Just after 9.15pm on this Wednesday evening, two Focke-Wulf Fw 190 single-engine fighter-bombers attacked at roof top level from east to west, each dropping one 1100lb (500kg) delayed action bomb, and strafing the town with cannon and machine-gun fire. One bomb exploded in the gardens at the rear of Nos 2-8 Grass Royal and Nos 13-16 Gordon Road, leaving a crater 5ft deep (1.5m) and 26ft (7.9m) wide. Although nearby houses were severely damaged, and several had to be rebuilt, two brick built reinforced surface air-raid shelters standing within 45ft (13.7m) of the centre of the bomb crater were reported to have stood up well to the explosion with no signs of roof movement or displacement of walls and only some surface fragmentation damage. The second bomb struck the ground between the Salvation Army Temple and the Central Junior School on Reckleford, bounced into the air and exploded in Dampier Street some 250 yards (229m) away. The shrapnel marks from this explosion can be seen on the east wall of the Yeovil Centre off Reckleford. The attack resulted in the deaths of three people and injuries to another 25, eight

of which were serious. Fifteen houses were destroyed or had to be demolished, and a further 972 were damaged. The people who lost their lives were:

Gordon Road/Grass Royal: Mr A. Mitchell and Mr A. Hussey
Dampier Street: Mrs E. Farwell

In the ten air raids on Yeovil, 107 high-explosive bombs and 18 oil fire bombs were dropped, 49 local people lost their lives and 122 were injured. 68 properties were destroyed and 2377 damaged. Only two bombs hit the Westland Aircraft Works.

HMS Hesperus

The ensign of the destroyer HMS *Hesperus* was laid up in St John's Church in January 1946 following her decommissioning at the end of the war. The destroyer was adopted by Yeovil and District in its National Savings 'Warship Week' in February 1942 after raising £425,000 which notionally covered its building cost. The ship was built by Thorneycroft, at Southampton in 1939 and was destined for the Brazilian Navy under the name *Juruena* but, on the outbreak of war in September 1939, the destroyer was requisitioned by the Royal Navy and named HMS *Hesperus* after the Greek name for the evening star. With a displacement of 1400 tons (1422 tonnes), *Hesperus* had a complement of 145 officers and men, and her armament consisted of three 4.7in (119mm) guns, one 3in (76mm) AA gun, and four 21in (533mm) torpedo tubes; later one of the guns was replaced by hedgehog depth charge projectors.

The *Hesperus* served most of the war in the North Atlantic where she was engaged on convoy escort duty. The role of the escort was vitally important in keeping the nation's supply lines open against German U-boat attacks. It was a long, tedious and very unpleasant task battling with the North Atlantic, often in fearsome weather and with the constant fear of U-boat attack. However *Hesperus* was a successful ship, and on convoy duty and in anti-submarine sweeps, she sank five U-boats and damaged several others. In one action, the destroyer brought the German U-357 to the surface by depth charge attack and then sank the enemy submarine by ramming it. The battle honours awarded to HMS *Hesperus* were: Norway 1940, Atlantic 1940-45 and English Channel 1945. In October 1993, a Civic Service of Remembrance and Dedication for the crew of HMS *Hesperus* was held at St John's Church followed by a parade and march-past. The ship's ensign can be seen in the church and the ship's crest is proudly displayed in the Mayor's Parlour in the Town House.

Iron railings and gates for the war effort

Ornamental iron railings and gates were a prominent feature of the front gardens of Yeovil residential areas built in the thirty or so years before 1914. Today, apart from iron stubs, few, if any, of the original railings and gates

86 The stubs of iron railings removed for the war effort in 1942. *Photo Jack W. Sweet*

remain. Towards the end of 1941, the Ministry of Supply ordered local authorities to carry out a survey of iron railings and gates in their areas, with the view to their removal to provide scrap iron for the war effort. Only railings and gates required for safety reasons, to enclose cattle or which had special artistic or historic merit, could be excluded. The completed schedule was sent to the Ministry of Works who employed contractors to carry out the removal. An article in the *Yeovil Review* for August 1942 explained how the railings and other iron material would help towards providing tanks and guns. A moderate sized garden gate would supply the metal parts to make five Bren guns, and 2cwt (101kg) of iron railings was equivalent in weight to two tank's radiators. In November 1942, the Borough Council was informed that the removal of all railings and gates had been completed, including those around St John's churchyard, Sidney Gardens and Bides Gardens, and the quantity of metal recovered amounted to 348 tons (354,000kg). The subsequent change in the appearance of many Yeovil streets resulting from the removal of the railings and gates, is one of the most lasting visual effects of the war *(86)*.

The British Restaurant

Early in the war, with the introduction of strict food rationing, the Government encouraged local authorities to establish publicly run British Restaurants to provide nutritious and inexpensive hot meals. In the autumn of 1941, the Borough Council decided to open and manage a British Restaurant in the Liberal Club in Middle Street, but problems with acquiring suitable equipment and appointing a suitable catering manager delayed the opening until 1 December 1942. Mrs D. Trump, from Newport, Monmouthshire, was the first and only manageress of the restaurant, which provided accommodation for 200 diners, each paying 1s for a two course hot meal and 1d for a cup of tea. Meals were served daily Monday to Saturday from noon to 2.00pm. The kitchen was well equipped with steam ovens and boilers as well as dishwashers and an electric potato peeler. The restaurant had a capacity of 1000 meals a day. 13,301 meals were served within the first two months and, by May 1943, the restaurant was self-supporting. In November 1944, the restaurant opened for teas on Friday and Saturday afternoons from 3.30 to 5.30pm. High tea cost 1s and plain tea 8d. The British Restaurant closed on 8 February 1947.

WAR MEMORIALS

The memorials to the fallen in both World Wars will be probably the most lasting visual remembrance of both conflicts. Likewise the headstones in the Commonwealth War Grave Commission Plot and other headstones in Yeovil Cemetery will remind generations to come of the sacrifice of the two World Wars.

The Yeovil war memorials

Shortly after the First World War broke out in August 1914, the Borough Council decided that there should be a memorial to honour those Yeovilians who gave their lives in the service of their country, but no one could have foreseen the terrible four years which would follow. However on 9 November 1918, two days before the Armistice brought the war to an end, the council resolved to take, 'The necessary steps to compile a list of all Yeovil officers and men who have fallen in the war, for the purpose of inscribing their names in a roll of honour for the Borough after the conclusion of hostilities'.

A War Memorial Committee was set up, the design finally agreed, and the council decided that the most appropriate site for the memorial was in the Borough. At 6 o'clock in the evening of Thursday 15 July 1921, the war memorial, with 226 names, was unveiled and dedicated before a large crowd of Yeovilians gathered in the Borough *(87)*. The 29ft high (8.8m) spire-shaped cross was designed by a Yeovil man, Mr Wilfred Childs, and made by Messrs Appleby and Childs a firm of Yeovil monumental masons, from the finest Ham Hill stone. The memorial was draped with the Union Flag and a White Ensign made by Miss M. Cooper and Miss Edith Childs. Describing the ceremony the *Western Gazette* reported:

> The Yeovil Territorial Company under the command of Captain J R Ware, marched in first and took up a position, and they were soon followed by a large contingent of ex-servicemen, headed by the Town Band, who marched in from Middle Street. These veterans,

87 The service of dedication of the war memorial in the Borough on 15 July 1921. *Photo from the collection of Jack W. Sweet*

many of who were wearing their medals, kept the ground – a hollow square before the flag covered cross - and with the police, did much towards preserving the quietude and order before the service. Then came a pathetic little procession into the square, a large party of children, many of them tiny tots, carrying posies of flowers, which they were to place later on the base of the Monument on which was engraved the names of their fathers. Just after the town clock struck the hour the final procession moved through the crowd. Headed by the clergy and ministers of all denominations it included the Mayor, and Aldermen and Councillors of Yeovil Corporation.

The hymn *Nearer My God to Thee* was sung and the Mayor, Alderman W.R.E. Mitchelmore, addressed the crowd. He said that the memorial was a token of love, respect and gratitude for the sacrifice made by those whose names were inscribed upon it and would be a shrine here in Yeovil for the men whose graves were scattered far and wide. At the call of the Mayor, Lieutenant Colonel F.D. Urwick, DSO, who had seen distinguished service with the Somerset Light Infantry in the Middle East, pulled a cord and the flags fell away. The Vicar of Yeovil then dedicated the memorial, a hymn and the National Anthem concluding the ceremony. Some years ago, the Town Council added to the memorial the names of those who fell in the Second World War, both service and civilian, and a young Yeovilian who died in the Falklands conflict in 1982.

In May 1946, the Borough Council decided that the most suitable form of memorial to remember the fallen of the Second World War, would be a public hall built on the pre-war proposed civic centre site at Hendford Manor. The Yeovil War Memorial Appeal raised £4,600, which was not enough to pay for the construction of a hall and in February 1952, the Borough Council agreed to hold the sum in trust towards 'the provision of a memorial hall within the ambit of the new Civic Centre when the public hall section of the Civic Centre is erected'. Three years later in February 1955, the Borough Council decided to commemorate Yeovilians who had died during the Second World War in the Forces, Civil Defence Services, and those civilians killed in the town during the bombing, by inscribing their names on a bronze memorial plaque. The council also decided that, when the memorial hall was built, the plaque should be placed in the building. However, pending the construction of the hall, the plaque was affixed to the wall of the council chamber in the Municipal Offices. The war memorial fund provided part of the cost of the Johnson Hall (the Octagon) where the plaque has been displayed since the Hall's completion in 1974.

The Yeovil and Sherborne memorial
In September 1994, following a service in St John's Church and a march-past

of Battle of Britain veterans and ex-servicemen and women, a commemorative plaque was unveiled on the side of Petters House in memory of the people of Yeovil and Sherborne who lost their lives in the bombing of the two towns in the Second World War.

The Preston Plucknett war memorial

Until the boundaries of the Borough of Yeovil were extended westward in 1928, Preston Plucknett was a separate parish, and at a parish meeting held in the school in October 1919, it was agreed that a war memorial cross should be placed in a prominent position in the village. A house-to-house collection raised the sum of £170 for the memorial, which took the form of a Ham stone cross, based on the design of a cross in the churchyard of Holy Trinity church, Shaftesbury. The memorial was placed in the orchard owned by Mr R. Ponsonby of Brympton D'Evercy and occupied by Mrs Hawkins, opposite the old post office and adjoining the road to Yeovil.

On Tuesday evening 6 July 1920, the memorial was dedicated in the presence of a large number of villagers and people from Yeovil. The cross standing on a rectangular block upon which was carved the names of the 15 men of the village who had lost their lives in the war, was made by the Ham Hill Company from its finest stone. A procession of 20 former soldiers, commanded by ex-Sergeant E.A. Stagg, left St James' church followed by the church choir, the Vicar of Yeovil-with-Preston, the Rev H.C. Sydenham, and churchwardens, and marched to the memorial where they formed a guard of honour around the cross which was draped with the Union Flag and the White

88 Left The wayside cross war memorial in Preston Plucknett. *Photo Jack W. Sweet*

89 Opposite The Commonwealth War Graves Commission Plot in Yeovil Cemetery. *Photo Jack W. Sweet*

Ensign. Following the singing of the hymn *Nearer My God to Thee* the flags were removed by two ex-servicemen, more hymns were sung, prayers led by the Vicar and several addresses were given. The service concluded with the National Anthem and the Last Post sounded by ex-Bugle-Major Donovan of Yeovil and ex-Private Beaton of East Coker. Flowers and wreaths were placed on the steps of the memorial and villagers and friends filed past. The names of two local men who died in the Second World War have also been inscribed on the war memorial, which was set back to its present position following road widening some years ago *(88)*.

Memorials to individuals

Fourteen soldiers who died in England during and immediately after the First World War are buried in Yeovil Cemetery, in individual plots or in family graves. A number of family headstones also commemorate sons who were killed on active service on the Western Front or in other theatres of the war. In 1917, Brigadier-General C.B. Prowse and Captain C.J. Prowse, RN, died on active service, and in the north aisle of St John's there is a magnificent stained glass window installed in 1917 in memory of the two brothers.

Early in the Second World War, a piece of ground in the cemetery was set aside by the Yeovil and Yeovil Without Joint Burial Committee, for service war burials. This Commonwealth War Graves Commission Plot, contains the graves of 30 soldiers, eleven of which were killed in the air raids on Houndstone Camp on 12 and 14 October 1940, and two men of The King's Own Scottish Borderers, who lost their lives in the bombing of the Corn

TO THE DEAR MEMORY OF
FRANK
BELOVED AND ONLY SON OF
F. AND N. ROSE.
KILLED BY ENEMY ACTION
OCT. 7TH. 1940.
AGED 17 YEARS 9 MONTHS.
HIS LIFE A BEAUTIFUL MEMORY
HIS DEATH A SILENT GRIEF.
TRANSLATED FROM THE WARFARE
OF THIS WORLD INTO GOD'S PEACE.
ALSO HIS MOTHER
NELLIE LUCY
CALLED TO REST JULY 4TH 1970.
AGED 82 YEARS.
DEARLY LOVED SADLY MISSED.
ALSO HIS FATHER
FREDERICK
CALLED TO REST
JANUARY 26TH 1982.
AGED 91 YEARS.
REUNITED.

90 Left The Rose family headstone commemorating the death of Frank Rose in the first air attack on Yeovil on 7 October 1940. *Photo Jack W. Sweet*

91 Opposite Westland Works photographed in February 1946. Note the air-raid shelters and several large buildings camouflaged to resemble houses. *Photo Westland Helicopters Ltd*

Exchange on Good Friday 1941 *(89)*. Elsewhere in the cemetery, in individual or family graves, are buried eight soldiers, five airmen, two sailors, and a member of the Home Guard – Volunteer Charles F. Langdon of 13th Gloucester (City of Bristol Battalion) Home Guard, killed in the bombing of the Bristol Aeroplane Company's factory at Filton, Bristol, on 25 September 1940. Many of the civilian casualties from the bombing of the town are buried in the cemetery and their headstones bear witness to their individual tragedies *(90)*. The three unknown persons who died in the bombing of the Preston Grove area on 8 October 1940 are buried together, marked with a headstone bearing the words 'October 1940 Three Air Raid Victims Known Unto God'.

WESTLAND AIRCRAFT

In April 1915, as the First World War entered its eighth month, the Minister for Munitions, Mr David Lloyd George, called for national action from industry to meet the acute and growing shortage of all kinds of munitions to fight the war. Messrs Petters Ltd, offered their Yeovil oil engine manufacturing facilities to the government, and from that decision, Westland Aircraft was born, and the future of Yeovil changed dramatically! The company's subsequent path has been extensively charted in a number of excellent books referred to in the Bibliography. However, the factory which grew up and remains the major employer and largest industrial complex in the town, retains many of the buildings constructed during the First and Second World Wars, albeit in modified forms and with different uses. The buildings or structures and their present uses are too numerous to detail in this work, but one example is the erecting shop built in 1939/40, and which is still used, suitably modified, for the Lynx and Merlin helicopter assembly lines. It can be seen in this aerial view of 1946 *(91)*. Westland manufactured 1100 aircraft in the First World War between 1915 and 1918, and throughout the Second, in addition to the Westland-designed Lysanders, Whirlwinds and Welkins, the firm built over 2400 aircraft to the designs of other companies, including Spitfires and Seafires. Because of the threat of air attack during the Second World War, Westland dispersed some of its operations to other parts of Yeovil and the surrounding district. Workshops for the manufacture of small parts were established underneath Messrs Vincents pre-war car park behind the former Odeon Cinema in

Court Ash; Petter's old Nautilus Works (now the First Bus Group garage) at Reckleford was used for storage of sheet metal and other equipment; and perishable, raw materials and rubber were stored in buildings now forming part of the Abbey Manor Trading Estate, off Stourton Way. Following company restructuring, Agusta Westland is now the world's largest manufacturer of helicopters, and perhaps remains the most powerful evidence and legacy of the effects of two World Wars on Yeovil and its people.

A TRIBUTE

This account of the remaining physical evidence of the World Wars has not sought to tell the history of Yeovil during the two momentous conflicts; that is another story. However, hundreds and thousands of local people strove to secure the victories which finally came; gave their time, their energies, and some the ultimate sacrifice, their lives or health. So, let us pay tribute to the Yeovil soldiers, sailors, airmen and women, home guard, observers, police, fire and ambulance services, medical services, civil defence, the welfare services, and all who rallied behind and supported the war effort and who have left no physical evidence of their efforts, other than perhaps the most important, the peace and security, albeit imperfect, we enjoy today.

APPENDIX I

92 Yeovil town centre, modified from the 1890 OS map. It shows the town plan before the twentieth century alterations

151

APPENDIX II

CHRONOLOGICAL LIST OF PRINCIPAL ARCHAEOLOGICAL ACTIVITY IN THE YEOVIL AREA

ABBREVIATIONS

Chronicle	*Chronicle: Journal of the Yeovil Archaeological & Local History Society*, followed by volume number
HER	Historic Environment Record number
JBAA	*Journal of the British Archaeological Association*, followed by volume number
N&QSD	*Notes and Queries for Somerset and Dorset*, followed by volume number
PSANHS	*Proceedings of the Somerset Archaeological and Natural History Society*, followed by volume number

DATE	LOCATION	OUTCOME	REFERENCE
1753	East Coker, north of Dunnock's Lane	Excavation of Roman villa	HER 53911; PSANHS, 65
1818 or 20	East Coker, north of Dunnock's Lane	Excavation of Roman villa and discovery of hunting mosaic	HER 53911; PSANHS, 65
1826	Stoford	Discovery of Bronze Age burials	HER 53549; PSANHS, 4
1860	West Coker	Excavation of barrow cemetery, Feebarrow	HER 54656; JBAA, 17
1861	West Coker, Chessels I	Excavation of Roman villa	HER 54658; JBAA, 18, 19
1909	Hendford Hill	Discovery of Bronze Age gold torc. Chance find	HER 54782; PSANHS, 55
*c.*1910	Larkhill	Discovery of Roman burials and associated finds	HER 54749; N&QSD, 11, 13
1916	Seaton Road	Discovery of Roman coin hoard	HER 15678, 54751; PSANHS, 62
1917	Westland I	Initial discovery of Roman pavement	PSANHS, 74
1920	St Michael's Avenue	Late Roman pottery	HER 55343; PSANHS, 74
1923	Yeovil, Pen Hill	Discovery of Roman pottery	HER 54744; PSANHS, 74
1920s	Westland II	Alderman Mitchelmore's initial investigation of Roman site	HER 54753
1927/28	Westland III	Professional excavation of Roman settlement	HER 15681, 16519, 54751; PSANHS, 74
1946-52	Lufton I	Roman villa excavation. YALHS	HER 53634; PSANHS, 97
1954-60	Ilchester Mead I	Excavation of Roman villa. YALHS	HER 53104; Hayward, 1982
1958	East Coker, Nash Lane	Excavation of Roman building. YALHS	HER 53910; PSANHS, 103
1958	West Coker, Chessels II	Excavation of Roman villa. YALHS	HER 15105; *Chronicle*, 5
1960-63	Lufton II	Roman villa excavations. YALHS	HER 53634; PSANHS, 116
1962	The George	Recording of fifteenth-century building during demolition. YALHS	PSANHS, 109

DATE	LOCATION	OUTCOME	REFERENCE
1969-72	Ilchester Mead II	Excavation of Roman villa. YALHS	HER 53104; Hayward, 1982
1972	Marks & Spencer	Town centre rescue watching brief. YALHS	
1974	West Coker, Chessels III	Excavation of Roman villa.	HER 15610
1975	Yew Tree Close Farm	Watching brief: Roman, Anglo-Saxon and medieval pottery found	HER 54759
1975/6	Penn Hill Park	Medieval pottery	HER 16485
1976	Odcombe	Survey of deserted medieval village	HER 54371; PSANHS, 121
1981	Odcombe	Survey of Five Ashes burial ground. YALHS	HER 54374
1983	Quedam	Discovery of post-medieval burials during building. YALHS	*Chronicle*, 2
1986	Middle Street, 56 & 58	Watching brief. YALHS. Nil result	HER 15178; PSANHS, 130
1980	Westland IV	Evaluation. Roman structures found	HER 15677; *Chronicle*, 7
1982	Wyndham Hill	Discovery of Bronze Age bronze axe-head	HER 16518; *Chronicle*, 7
1986	Library Site I	Town centre rescue site. Medieval and post medieval material. YALHS	HER 12292; *Chronicle*, 3
1987	St Gilda's Convent	Watching brief, mostly nineteenth century. YALHS	HER 15548; PSANHS, 132
1987	Library Site II	Town centre rescue site. Medieval and post-medieval material. YALHS	HER 15550; *Chronicle*, 4
1987	Petters House	Town centre rescue site. Medieval and post-medieval material. YALHS	HER 15549; *Chronicle*, 4
1987	Odcombe	Five Ashes Non-Conformist burial ground. Recording during clearance of undergrowth. YALHS	HER 54374; *Chronicle*, 4
1987	East Coker I	Rescue excavation on late medieval house site. YALHS	HER 44878; *Chronicle*, 4
1987	Westfield Avenue	Discovery of Roman pottery and bone during landscaping	HER 57177; *Chronicle*, 4, 8
1987	Belmont Street	Discovery of Anglo-Saxon Ham stone baluster	HER 15503, 15511; *Chronicle*, 4
1988	Horsey Lane	Watching brief, nothing found	HER 90088
1988	South Street	Town centre rescue watching brief, nineteenth century. YALHS	*Chronicle*, 4
1988	West Coker, Chessels IV	Small evaluation of Roman villa. Mid Iron Age to fourth century AD	HER 15494; PSANHS, 132
1988	Church House	Recording medieval worked stone. YALHS	HER 15545; PSANHS, 132
1989	Lloyds Bank	Town centre rescue site. Medieval and post-medieval material. YALHS	*Chronicle*, 4
1989	Town House	Photographic survey prior to conversion. YALHS	*Chronicle*, 4
1989	Ninesprings	Examination of Leisure Pool site during groundwork. Nil result. YALHS	
1989	Great Lyde Farm	Discovery of Roman pottery.	*Chronicle*, 4
1990	East Coker II	Trial excavation on late medieval house site. YALHS	HER 44877; *Chronicle*, 5
1990	Lysander Road	Observation of pipeline across possible course of Roman road. Nil result. YALHS	HER 15658; PSANHS, 134
1990	Stoford, Hooper's Lane	Evaluation found traces of medieval occupation	HER 55861
1990	Reckleford (Esso garage)	Observation during construction work. Nil result. YALHS	
1991	Tesco site, Huish	Exhumation of bodies from Paradise burial ground, prior to building work	HER 15716; PSANHS, 135
1991	Stoford I	Trial excavation prior to building work. Stone-built features, post-medieval pot. YALHS	HER 15714; *Chronicle*, 5
1991	A37, pipeline south of Ilchester	Observation during digging. Concentration of clay pipes, many of which were stamped 'ID'. Late-seventeenth century. YALHS	*Chronicle*, 5

DATE	LOCATION	OUTCOME	REFERENCE
1992	West Hendford	Attempt to delineate south boundary of Westland site and Roman road. No Roman material found, only 1 sherd of medieval pot	HER 57057
1992	Lysander Road	Nil result	HER 90031
c.1992	Forest Hill	Discovery of flint tools	HER 16489
1994	Stoford II	Excavation on garden site. Worked flint, medieval and post-medieval pot. YALHS	HER 55862; *Chronicle*, 6
1996	Assessment Report	Archaeological Assessment of Yeovil carried out and written up. Somerset County Council	
1996	Yeovil, St John's	Observation of area below floor level, close to font. Nineteenth-century grave slab recorded. YAHLS	*Chronicle*, 7
1996	West of Odcombe	Pipeline watching brief. Prehistoric material found over most of route and a medieval settlement	HER 55425
1997	North Coker Mill	Discovery of skeleton (possibly modern) and Roman pottery	HER 56945
1997	Stoford III	Excavation on garden site, discovery of boundary ditch, worked flint, medieval pottery. YALHS	HER 15112; *Chronicle*, 7
1998	Church House	Investigation found sixteenth to eighteenth-century material and undated wall foundations	HER 57197
1998	Princes Street	Cobbled yard above layer containing late nineteenth-century pottery, sands below discoloured but no dating evidence	HER 90111
1998	East Coker	Watching brief found pottery, ditches and pits dating from twelfth-seventeenth century	HER 56949
1998	Chantry	Observation and recording during demolition of wall. YALHS	*Chronicle*, 7
1999	Stoford IV	Assessment prior to building, post-medieval ditches and pit, possibly medieval burnt layer	HER 57040
1999	Town House	Eighteenth and nineteenth-century refuse pits, natural below layer with modern material and brick	HER 35971
1999	44/46 Middle Street	Only natural	HER 44955
1999	Mermaid	Eastern part of site evidence of tanning and eighteenth-century pot, perhaps dumped	HER 35943
2000	Alvington Lane	Worked flint and Roman pottery and hearth	HER 11636
2000	Alvington	Investigation found late Iron Age and Roman pottery. Likely to have been site of farmstead throughout period	HER 11305
2001	Alvington Lane	Post-medieval features, flint and Roman from topsoil	HER 11694
2001	Alvington	Gully and other features, Radiocarbon date: 1900-1100 BC Bronze Age settlement	HER 11642
2001	Penfield Gospel Hall	Seventeenth century onwards	HER 15932
2001	Westland V	Investigation ahead of proposed building development. Nothing found	
2001	Freedom Avenue	Roman Black Burnished pottery and possible wall	HER 15038
2002	Preston Road	No finds earlier than eighteenth century	HER 15891
2002	Baptist church	Southern part of site had late medieval and seventeenth to mid-eighteenth century material. North-eastern part barren, possibly removed by earlier construction.	HER 15472
2002	West Street	Observation during demolition of WWII air-raid shelters. YALHS	*Chronicle*, 8
2003	Westland VI	Preliminary investigation ahead of construction of new play area. Nil result	HER 16332
2003	Middle Street	Observation during water main renewal. Stone structures close to site of The George. YALHS	*Chronicle*, 8
2003	Westland VII	Observation during water main renewal. YALHS	*Chronicle*, 8

BIBLIOGRAPHY

Abdy, A., 2002 *Romano-British Coin Hoards*. Shire.

Allen-Brown, R., 1969 *The Normans and the Norman Conquest*. Constable.

Anon., 1853 'The Museum', *Proceedings of the Somerset Archaeological and Natural History Society*, 4, 8-9.

Ashdown, P., 1993 'Two Sheila-na-Gigs at Stoke-sub-Hamdon', *Proceedings of the Somerset Archaeological and Natural History Society*, 137, 67-74.

Aston, M., and Burrow, I., (eds) 1982 *The Archaeology of Somerset*, Somerset County Council.

Aston, M., 1984 'The Towns of Somerset', in Haslam, J., 1984.

Barker, K., 1984 'Sherborne in Dorset', *Anglo-Saxon Studies in Archaeology and History*, 3.

— 1985/6 'Pen, Ilchester and Yeovil', *Proceedings of the Somerset Archaeological and Natural History Society*, 130.

Batten, J., 1894 *Historical Notes on Parts of South Somerset*. Whitby & Son.

— 1898 'An Early Chapter of the History of Yeovil', *Proceedings of the Somerset Archaeological and Natural History Society*, XLIV, 4.

Blair, J., 1988 'From Minster to Parish Church', in Blair J. (ed.) 1988.

— (ed.), 1988 *Minsters and Parish Churches*, Oxford University Committee for Archaeology, Monograph No.17.

Bri   ce, M.H., 1984 *Stronghold: A history of military architecture*. Batsford Ltd.

Brooke, L., 1978 *The Book of Yeovil*. Barracuda Books.

— 1979 *Street Names in Yeovil*. Yeovil Archaeological and Local History Society.

— (ed.), 1981 *Yeovil: the changing scene*. Yeovil Archaeological and Local History Society.

— 1986 'Robert de Sambourne', *Chronicle*, 3, 80.

— 1991 'Two 14th Century Documents in the Museum of South Somerset', *Chronicle*, 5, 48.

— 1993 'The Story of a Hill – Hendford Hill, Yeovil', *Chronicle*, 6, 8.

— 1995 'Wyndham Hill', *Chronicle*, 6, 95.

— 1996 'Why Was It Called That – A Study of Some Yeovil Field Names: Part 1', *Chronicle*, 7, 8.

— 1997 'A Study of Some Yeovil Field-Names – Part 2', *Chronicle*, 7, 33.

Coleman-Smith, R. and Pearson, E., 1988 *Excavations in the Donyatt Potteries*. Phillimore.

Collinson, J., 1791 *The History and Antiquities of the County of Somerset*, Vol.3, (reprinted 1983, Alan Sutton).

Darvill, T., 1987 *Prehistoric Britain*. Batsford.

de la Bédoyère, G., 1991 *The Buildings of Roman Britain*. Batsford.

D'Maurney Gibbons, K., 1995 *A Path to the Door – The Complete Petter History*. Alan Sutton Publishing in association with Lister-Petter Ltd.

Dunning, R.W. (ed.), 1974 *The Victoria County History of Somerset, III*.

Dunning, R.W., 1975 'Ilchester: A Study in Continuity', *Proceedings of the Somerset Archaeological and Natural History Society*, 119, 44.

— 1976 'The Minster at Crewkerne', *Proceedings of the Somerset Archaeological and Natural History Society*, 120.

Eogan, G., 1967 'The associated finds of gold bar torcs', *The Journal of the Royal Society of Antiquaries of Ireland*, 97, 129-175.

Gerard, T., 1900 *Particular Description of the County of Somerset*, 1633, Somerset Record Society, 15.

Gerrard, J., 1997, 'The Wyndham Hill Axehead', *Chronicle*, 7, 48-49.

— 2001 'Romano-British coarsewares from Westfield Avenue, Yeovil, Somerset', *Chronicle*, 8, 63-66.

— and Mills, S., 2001 'The Architectural and Geophysical Investigation of a Possible Apsidal Chancel at the Church of St Mary the Virgin, Stoke sub Hamdon, Somerset', *Chronicle*, 8, 60-62.

— 2002 'An Anglo-Saxon Spur from Yeovil', *Chronicle*, 8, 76-77.

Gittos, B. and M., 1988 'Recent Archaeology in Yeovil: Belmont Street', *Chronicle*, 4, 53.

— 1989 'Archaeological Unit Report: Lloyds Bank', *Chronicle*, 4, 122-124.

— 1989 'Archaeological Unit Report: Nethercoombe Farm, Sherborne', *Chronicle*, 4, 125-127.

— 1989 'Archaeological Unit Report: Nethercoombe Farm, Sherborne', *Chronicle*, 4, 153-154.

— 1989 'The Evidence for the Saxon Minster at Yeovil', *Chronicle*, 4, 95-104

— 1991 'Notes on Alvington's Archaeological Potential', *Chronicle*, 5, 94.

— 1991 'The Surviving Anglo-Saxon Fabric of East Coker Church', *Proceedings of the Somerset Archaeological and Natural History Society*, 135, 107-111.

— 1994 'Archaeological Unit Report: Stoford', *Chronicle*, 6, 78-9.

— 1995 'Records Relating to the Yeovil Area in the Early 14th Century', *Chronicle*, 6, 90-93.

— 1997 'Excavations at Stoford, 1994 & 1997', *Chronicle*, 7, 67-72.

Golding, B., 1990 'Robert of Mortain', *Anglo-Norman Studies,* 13, 119-140.

Goodchild, J., Hayward, L.C. and Batty, E.A, 1954 *The Borough of Yeovil*. Mayor Alderman and Burgesses of Yeovil.

Harvey, J., 1984 *English Mediaeval Architects*, (2nd edition). Alan Sutton.

Haslam, J., (ed.), 1984 *Anglo-Saxon Towns in Southern England*. Phillimore.

Hawkins, M., 1988 *Somerset at War 1939-1945*. The Dovecote Press.

Hayward, L.C., 1952 'The Roman villa at Lufton, near Yeovil', *Proceedings of the Somerset Archaeological and Natural History Society*, 116, 59-77.

— 1965 'The George Hotel Yeovil Somerset', *Proceedings of the Somerset Archaeological and Natural History Society*, 109, 84-97.

— 1972 'The Roman Villa at Lufton, near Yeovil', *Proceedings of the Somerset Archaeological and Natural History Society*, 97, 91-112.

— 1978 *The Romans in Ilchester, Lufton, Yeovil and district*, Yeovil Archaeological and Local History Society.

— 1982 *Ilchester Mead Roman Villa*, Ilchester Occasional Papers, 31.

— 1984 'The Quedam Tomb', *Chronicle*, 2, 81-2.

— 1987 *From Portreeve to Mayor*. Castle Cary Press.

— and Brooke, L., 1980 *Bygone Yeovil*. Yeovil Archaeological and Local History Society.

Higham, N., 1997 *The Death of Anglo-Saxon England*. Sutton Publishing.

Holmes, T.S., (ed.), 1896 *The Register of Ralph of Shrewsbury*, Somerset Record Society, 10.

James, D.N., 1997 *Westland – The Archive Photographs Series*. Chalford Publishing Company.

— 2002 *Westland – A History*. Tempus Publishing Ltd.

Leach, P., 2001 *Roman Somerset*. Dovecote Press.

Leland, J., (ed. by Toulmin Smith, L.), 1964 *Itinerary of John Leland*. Centaur Press.

Leech, R. and Leach, P., 1982 'Roman town and countryside, 43-450 AD', in Aston, M. and Burrow, I., 1982.

Mills, S., 2003 'The Mysterious Dragonslayer Window', *Chronicle*, 8, 111-113.

Moore, J., 1861 'On some ancient remains discovered at West Coker, Somersetshire', *Journal of the British Archaeological Association*, 17, 288-289.

Ordnance Survey, reprinted 1993, *Yeovil East 1901*. Alan Godfrey Maps.

— 1994, *Yeovil West 1901*. Alan Godfrey Maps.

Parker-Pearson, M., 1993 *Bronze Age Britain*. Batsford.

Radford, C., 1928 'The Roman site at Westland', *Proceedings of the Somerset Archaeological and Natural History Society*, 74, 122-143.

St George Gray, H., 1909 'The gold torc found at Yeovil, 1909', *Proceedings of the Somerset Archaeological and Natural History Society*, 55, 66-84.

— 1916 'Hoard of Roman coins found at Yeovil', *Proceedings of the Somerset Archaeological and Natural History Society*, 62, 86-110.

— 1930 'Inscription to Flavius Valerius Severus found at Stoke-under-Ham', *Proceedings of the Somerset Archaeological and Natural History Society*, 76 , 19-21.

Salway, P., 1981 *Roman Britain*. Oxford University Press.

Sarkar, D., *Angriff Westland*. Ramrod Publications.

Silcox, E., 1978 'Looking Back', *Chronicle*, 1.

Taylor, H.M. and J., 1980 *Anglo-Saxon Architecture*. Cambridge University Press.

Thorn, C. and F., (eds), 1980 *Domesday Book 8: Somerset*. Phillimore.

Watkiss, L. and Chibnall, M., 1994 *The Waltham Chronicle*. Clarendon Press.

Weaver, F.W., (ed.), 1903 *Somerset Mediaeval Wills*, Somerset Record Society, 19, 287.

Whitelock, D., (ed.), 1930 *Anglo-Saxon Wills*. Cambridge University Press.

Williams, A. and Martin, G., (eds), 2002 *Domesday Book: A Complete Translation*. Penguin Books.

Wills, H., 1985 *Pill Boxes: a study of U.K. defences 1940*. Leo Cooper.

INDEX